THE I

POPE
JOHN
PAUL II

THE LEGACY OF
POPE
JOHN
PAUL II

His Contribution
to Catholic Thought

JOHN F. CROSBY, RUSSELL HITTINGER,
JOSEPH W. KOTERSKI, DAVID L. SCHINDLER,
AND WILLIAM B. SMITH

Edited by Geoffrey Gneuhs

A Herder & Herder Book
The Crossroad Publishing Company
New York

The Crossroad Publishing Company
370 Lexington Avenue, New York, NY 10017

Printed in the United States of America

Library of Congress Cataloging-in-Publication Data
The legacy of John Paul II: his contribution to Catholic thought / John F. Casey ... [et
  al.] ; edited by Geoffrey Gneuhs.
    p. cm.
  "A Herder & Herder book."
  Includes bibliographical references.
  ISBN 0-8245-1831-4
  1. John Paul II, Pope, 1920– 2. Catholic Church – History – 20th century. I. Crosby,
John F., 1944– II. Gneuhs, Geoffrey.
  BX1378.5. L43 2000
  230′.2′092 – dc21
                                                                99-053600

1 2 3 4 5 6 7 8 9 10   06 05 04 03 02 01 00

Contents

Introduction

To assess the abiding legacy of Pope John Paul II, the authors of this volume have needed to attend both to the stage of world diplomacy and to the heart of the Church. In the fall of Communism, for instance, one can see his hand planting and nurturing the idea for the Solidarity movement. In the promulgation of the new Code of Canon Law, the *Catechism of the Catholic Church*, and a series of weighty encyclicals, one can see his hand crafting a decisive interpretation of Vatican II and completing the renewal of the Church which that Council began.

His labors as Pope have been pastoral and intellectual. With missionary zeal he has announced a new evangelization, and his numerous visits to countries around the globe have provided personal example of how to carry out this special effort to reawaken faith in cultures whose Christianity has been fading. At the same time, with a scholar's solitude he has authored profound works on fundamental moral theology and its application to today's most pressing life questions. In support of all these ventures, he offers his own religious and philosophical synthesis of traditional Thomism and contemporary personalism.

The introductory essay in this collection surveys the variety of forms which his writing has taken, from plays and poetry to philosophical treatises, catechetical lessons, and encyclical letters. It groups his magisterial pronouncements around four themes: (1) reflection on Christ's work of redemption and the restoration of human dignity, considered in light of the community of persons in the Trinity; (2) articulation of a social ethics that offers a fresh interpretation of the principles of solidarity and subsidiarity as a possible solution to the social problems of our day; (3) concern with such pastoral problems as the healing of divisions within the Church and the discernment of authentic and inauthentic strategies for evangelization and missionary efforts; (4) elaboration of a scripturally based and philosophically sound moral theology, one which gives pride of place to the personalist norm in its supple but firm application to such difficult questions as abortion, euthanasia, and capital punishment.

The essays by William Smith and John Crosby then study the Pope's thought on moral theology in further detail, while the essays by Russell Hittinger and David Schindler consider his views on social ethics and contemporary culture.

In the areas of moral theology, canon law, and catechesis, John Paul's work, argues William Smith, exhibits a development in profound continuity with previous popes and with Vatican II. In particular, he has provided a fruitful example of what Vatican II called for in the renewal of moral theology by using scripture not for proof-texting but for providing in the person of Christ the abiding "truth about man" that God has revealed to be the authentic guide for resolving moral questions. Smith emphasizes John Paul's defense of certain theses that many of his critics find most difficult to accept, including the uniqueness of Christ ("this is not just another Buddha") and the paradox that the vocation of every Christian is to find one's own salvation precisely by the sincere gift of oneself in committed love for others. Against the vacuity of moral relativism and the excessive claims sometimes made for individual autonomy, Smith explains the Pope's view that human freedom is best preserved (not alienated) by obedience to God and the truths about morality that God has established for humanity.

John Crosby argues for the intellectual leadership that John Paul's initiatives have provided, not only on such broad topics as conscience, freedom, and law, but on such particular issues as the basic equality of man and woman in marriage. The Pope's careful reflections on how the image of the triune God is present in the difference between man and woman offers, for Crosby, a corrective to contrasting errors frequent in contemporary thought. In some cases there is a materialist reduction of the person to just the body, whereas in other quarters a neo-Manichean aversion to the body reduces the body to a mere instrument, taken to be available for any and every sort of manipulation as if it were but raw material. Instead, the Pope offers a theology of the body as essential to the expression of the whole person and endowed with a "nuptial meaning" that can already be read in the creation accounts of Genesis and that is seen restored and renewed in Christ.

It is not simply that John Paul II has a predilection for this area of thought; rather, one gets the impression that his own long dedication to the study of these issues, from his 1961 book *Love and Responsibility* through the four-year series of Wednesday Catecheses early in his papacy, has been providentially guided so as to provide the Church with an articulate representative in one of the most hotly contested areas of morality, and yet an area subject to such frequent misunderstanding precisely because even the most well-meaning of moralists find sexuality and human relations such a delicate subject. For John Paul, the mystery of the human person needs to be contemplated in the light of the biblical theology of the body in order to bring out the Christian meaning of human sexuality and to shed adequate light on the universal vocation of all humanity that consists in the sincere gift of the self.

Russell Hittinger's essay traces John Paul's social thought against the dual problematic of the modern state and the industrial revolution. Since the time of the French Revolution, popes have identified this pair of concerns as the proper matrix of social thought and in a long series of encyclicals they have developed a consistent analysis of the nature of the problem, but its resolution has been perplexing, especially since the demise of even the vestiges of the old "Christendom" with the fall of the last Christian kingdoms by the end of the World War I. By showing the historical background, Hittinger exhibits an important source for John Paul's emphasis on human solidarity, namely, the steady obliteration of those social and cultural forms in which Christian solidarity had traditionally been embedded. The development of the modern state has been a kind of revolution from above that has generated a social atomism in which individuals are more isolated, deprived of the support of many of the older mediating institutions, and thereby kept relatively weaker before the power of the state. The industrial revolution, on the other hand, has been a kind of revolution from below, for it has made possible a mass society of unprecedented size.

After tracing the zig-zags of papal policy for the last century and a half, a policy that sometimes criticized the state for exercising too much power but sometimes chided the state for not using enough of its power to remedy social ills, Hittinger makes the case that the recurrent papal analysis of the problem has been both accurate and consistent, for it has objected to the trend in modern regimes to make public things that deserve to be private and to privatize things that ought to be public. These trends have been, Hittinger avers, the result of a basic error: the repudiation of any natural or supernatural good in favor of seeing the political common good as merely a creation of the human will — the clever fiction championed by social contract theory, which holds that the social order, like the political order, is only an instrument for satisfying the interests of the contracting parties.

The resolution of the problem, however, is another matter. Hittinger sees John Paul as continuing and developing the opening that Pope Pius XII made toward considering the previously suspect notion of constitutional democracy as *a* (but not *the*) legitimate means for social order. Relying on the distinction worked out by Jacques Maritain between the instrumentalist and substantive conceptions of the state, Hittinger shows that John Paul's *Centesimus Annus*, with its focus on the transcendent dignity of the human person as the primary subject of rights, enunciates a vision of the social order that would weaken the power of the state by progressively expanding the chain of social solidarity. Whether this new vision will in fact take hold, Hittinger observes, remains a question for future historians.

David Schindler takes up the question of the cultural implementation of the Pope's vision from another angle. If the Pope's Christ-centered vision of the human person and society is to be realized, a new evangelization will need to transform the cultural situation prevalent today. After providing a careful review of the distinctive interpretation that the Pope has been endeavoring to place on the relation of the Church to the modern world that Vatican II's *Gaudium et Spes* initiated, Schindler analyzes the particular theological cast of the new evangelization for which the Pope has called. It is especially directed toward remedying the culture of death that the diverse forms of "practical atheism" currently operative in the world have induced, especially by a quasi-Pelagian expectation of using technological means to resolving every problem, with little or no thought for the intrinsically subjective matrix of human society. In short, human "problems" cannot be solved by power alone but will need to concentrate on the engagement of personal freedom, individual restraint, and responsibility to one's community to be fully satisfying. For Pope John Paul II, Schindler reminds us, this means thoroughly considering society and the human person in the light of the mystery of the communion of the divine Trinity.

JOSEPH W. KOTERSKI, S.J.
Fordham University

Chapter 1

An Introduction to the Thought of Pope John Paul II

JOSEPH W. KOTERSKI

So many words have come from the pen of the Holy Father! Best known perhaps are the encyclicals that Pope John Paul II has written.[1] But there are also various other kinds of papal documents that bear not just his formal authorship but his personal touch, including the speeches and sermons he has delivered in an incredible host of languages.[2] Then

---

JOSEPH W. KOTERSKI, S.J., is Associate Professor of Philosophy at Fordham University, Bronx, New York.

1. An encyclical is a letter by the Pope, traditionally addressed to all the bishops of the Church, but since John XXIII, often addressed to a broader public, such as "all people of good will." An "apostolic constitution" is a papal document presented in solemn form with a legal content dealing with issues of faith, doctrine, or discipline that are important for the universal Church or a specific diocese. Other categories of papal writing include "apostolic letters" (on various topics and addressed to more specialized groups than encyclicals), "apostolic exhortations" (reflections by the Pope on the topics that have been the subject of the triennial Synod of Bishops), and "instructions" (statements of clarification, often on very technical points, such as regulations for the proper conduct of the liturgy or the moral evaluation of new medical techniques like *in vitro* fertilization).

2. There is a special hermeneutic problem in dealing with papal writings. How much is properly the Pope's own and how much is written for him by others? The process of composition of such documents is often quite complex. Important as this scholarly question is, there will be no attempt here to resolve it for the writings of John Paul II. Yet it is possible to make the general observation that even in documents that give most evidence of composition by committee, the personal tone characteristic of this Pope regularly breaks through. Since he has assumed responsibility for these writings, they will simply be taken as manifestations of his own mind for the purposes of this essay.

there are his books, some written before he assumed the pontificate[3] and some since then, some intended for a very broad audience, others with the abstractions that only a philosopher could love. The scope of his thought, let alone its profundity, could easily make it seem impossible ever to digest what he has written, even supposing that one could manage to read it all.

John Paul II's Coat-of-Arms

As a point of entry into his thought, we might reflect on the coat-of-arms that Pope John Paul II has chosen for his pontificate. His crest contains a large cross, and in the lower right corner a prominent M — the Cross of Christ and an *M* for Mary. To the mystery of the Cross of Christ, he returns again and again as he progressively unfolds the central theoretical support for his expansive vision, a theological anthropology centered around the theme that it is Christ who reveals man to himself. It is a religious vision of humanity as so deeply loved by the Creator that the Word of God became incarnate in order to redeem us by His suffering and death. From the moment of his first encyclical, *Redemptor Hominis* in 1979, John Paul has offered us a sustained meditation on the mystery of the redemption.

In one sense there is absolutely nothing new here or in any of the other venues in which he has sounded this theme ever since. It is simply the truth of the Gospel. But to a world that has forgotten the splendor of such truth, John

---

3. To date, the best study of the prepapal writings is Rocco Buttiglione's *Karol Wojtyla: The Thought of the Man Who Became Pope John Paul II* (Grand Rapids: Eerdmans, 1997), trans. Paolo Guietti and Francesca Murphy from *Il pensiero di Karol Wojtyla* (Milan: Jaca, 1982). For an insightful study of both John Paul II's papal and prepapal thought, and especially for the significance of the plays which he has composed, see Kenneth L. Schmitz, *At the Center of the Human Drama: The Philosophical Anthropology of Karl Wojtyła/Pope John Paul II* (Washington, D.C.: Catholic University of America Press, 1993).

Paul's distinctive way of representing this truth of Christianity has served to renew and restore this splendor. In contrast to the way in which Thomas Aquinas started his *Summa Theologiae,* the anthropological turn of John Paul's thought is typically modern. In fact, this is one important aspect of *Fides et Ratio,* the encyclical released in the fall of 1998. How many times has John Paul chanted "Be Not Afraid!" to audiences of hundreds of thousands, and how many times have his listeners heard a line from the Gospel as if they had never heard it before. Even the most hardened and cynical among secular reporters have been known to grow suddenly mushy. Yet his message is not sentimental. It is delivered by someone with a mastery of the modern communications media and with a sense of the significance of his office upon the world stage, someone who loved being an actor in his youth and who has written plays of his own. But the message goes far beyond the admittedly enchanting medium. Often it is a hard message, for the center of the message, like the center of the crest, is the Cross of Christ.

The *M* that is so prominent on the papal crest is the Marian *M,* and the Blessed Mother is never far from John Paul's focus. Like the fascinating set of Pietàs in the gallery under the church that he forced the authorities to allow in Nowa Huta,[4] the Pope's vision of the Blessed Mother is especially marked by suffering and by faith. As he explains in *Redemptoris Mater,* the Church needs to remain steadfastly united to the sufferings of humanity, just as Mary in the Pietà accepts and embraces the sufferings of her Son. In faith she mourns His brutal death but in confident prayer she awaits His resurrection and glory.

The pair of symbols that John Paul placed on his papal crest can help us to focus our attention in this introduc-

---

4. A church built in the shape of Noah's Ark that then Archbishop Karol Wojtyla had to force the Communist authorities to accept when they tried to exclude any place of worship from a model new socialist suburb being created for Krakow's steelworkers.

tion to his thought. What he has accomplished on the stage of the world and within the Church flows directly from a vision of the Church, renewed in Christ, challenging the world to a new respect for human dignity. This vision is evident in all the main areas of his activity. It is prominent in the call to solidarity that sparked the Solidarity movement in Poland and the ferment, spiritual and social, that led to the demise of the Communist regime in 1989. He has vigorously fostered a dialogue between faith and culture, contributing broadly, including three encyclicals on the reconstruction of the economic order, an important document on the theory of evolution, and the public rehabilitation of Galileo, a gesture of enormous symbolic importance in the reconciliation of science and religion. This vision is also manifest in his concern for the inner unity of the Church that has brought him to such acts as the promulgation of the new Code of Canon Law in 1983 and the completion of the renewal of the Church's liturgical books (a project mandated by Vatican Council II), not to mention the publication of the long-needed *Catechism of the Catholic Church* (1994), the steady but delicate work of papal outreach to the Orthodox churches, and the preparation for the third millennium by the proclamation of a "new evangelization."

The Major Categories of John Paul's Writings

Before undertaking some thematic comments on the vast compass of John Paul's thought, it may prove helpful to review the major categories of his writing and to list some of the important works of each type. The diverse styles in which he is accustomed to express himself show him to possess great artistic sensibility as well as the mastery of such difficult techniques as modern biblical exegesis, phenomenological inquiry, and Thomistic distinctions; he is both a tender confessor and a bold political thinker.

A Partial List of the Writings of Pope John Paul II

Drama and Poetry

Collected Poems. Trans. with introductory essay and notes by Jerzy Peterkiewicz. New York: Random House, 1979, 1982.

The Collected Plays and Writings on Theater. Trans. Boleslaw Taborski. Berkeley: University of California Press, 1987.

Prepapal Books

The Acting Person. Rev. ed. 1977. Trans. Andrzej Potocki. 1979.

Sign of Contradiction. New York: Seabury Press, 1979. A retreat preached to Paul VI and his curia.

Sources of Renewal: The Implementation of Vatican II. Trans. P. S. Falla. 1980.

Faith according to St. John of the Cross. Trans. Jordan Aumann. San Francisco: Ignatius Press, 1981.

Love and Responsibility. Trans. H. T. Willetts. 1981.

Lubliner Vorlesungen, 1954–57. Ed. Juliusz Stroynowski. Stuttgart-Degerloch: Seewald, 1981.

Encyclicals

Redemptor Hominis, The Redeemer of Man (1979)

Dives in Misericordia, On the Mercy of God (1980)

Laborem Exercens, On Human Work (1981)

Slavorum Apostoli, Apostles to the Slavs (1985)

Dominum et Vivificantem, The Lord and Giver of Life (1986)

Redemptoris Mater, Mother of the Redeemer (1987)

Sollicitudo Rei Socialis, On Social Concern (1987)

Redemptoris Missio, On the Mission of the Redeemer (1990)

Centesimus Annus, On the Hundredth Anniversary of *Rerum Novarum* (1991)

Veritatis Splendor, The Splendor of Truth (1993)

Evangelium Vitae, The Gospel of Life (1995)

Ut Unum Sint, That They May Be One (1995)

Fides et Ratio, On Faith and Reason (1998)

Apostolic Constitutions, Exhortations, Letters, Instructions

Catechesi Tradendae, Apostolic Exhortation on Catechesis in Our Time (1979)

Sapientia Christiana, Apostolic Constitution on Ecclesiastical Universities and Faculties (1979)

Inestimabile Donum, Instruction concerning Worship of the Eucharistic Mystery (1980)

Dominica Cenae, On the Mystery and Worship of the Eucharist (1980)

Familiaris Consortio, Apostolic Exhortation on the Family (1981)

Redemptionis Donum, The Gift of the Redemption (1984)

Salvifici Doloris, Apostolic Letter on the Christian Meaning of Human Suffering (1984)

Reconciliatio et Paenitentia, Apostolic Exhortation on Reconciliation and Penance (1984)

Duodecimum Saeculum, Apostolic Letter on the Twentieth Century (1987)

Mulieris Dignitatem, Apostolic Letter on the Dignity and Vocation of Women (1988)

Christifideles Laici, Apostolic Exhortation on the Vocation and Mission of the Lay Faithful in the Church and in the World (1988)

Ecclesia Dei, Apostolic Letter on the 25th Anniversary of the Constitution on the Sacred Liturgy (1988)

On the Occasion of the Marian Year, Apostolic Letter (1988)

Euntes in Mundum, Apostolic Letter, Go into All the World (1988)

Redemptoris Custos, Apostolic Exhortation on the Guardian of the Redeemer, St. Joseph (1989)

Ex Corde Ecclesiae, Apostolic Constitution, From the Heart of the Church (1990)

Pastores Dabo Vobis, Apostolic Exhortation, I Will Give You Shepherds (1992)

Letter To Families (1994)

Tertio Millennio Adveniente, Apostolic Letter on the Third Millennium (1994)

Letter to Women (1995)

Orientale Lumen, Apostolic Letter, Light of the East (1995)

Vita Consecrata, Apostolic Exhortation on the Consecrated Life (1996)

Universi Dominici Gregis, Apostolic Constitution on the Vacancy of the Apostolic See and the Election of the Roman Pontiff (1996)

Books and Other Writings from the Papal Period

Fruitful and Responsible Love. New York: Seabury Press, 1979. His 1978 address on the tenth anniversary of *Humanae Vitae*, with contributions by various respondents.

Holy Thursday Letters to My Brother Priests. Each year from 1979.

The Original Unity of Man and Woman. Lectures on Genesis (1979–80).

Blessed Are the Pure of Heart. Lectures on the Sermon on the Mount and on St. Paul (1980–81).

Massimiliano Kolbe, patrono del nostro difficile secolo. Vatican City: Libreria editrice vaticana, 1982.

"Be Not Afraid!" — André Frossard in Conversation with Pope John Paul II. Trans. from the French (1982) J. R. Foster. London: The Bodley Head, 1984.

Reflections on Humanae Vitae. Lectures on *Humanae Vitae* (1984).

The Theology of Marriage and Celibacy: Catechesis on Marriage and Celibacy. Boston: Daughters of St. Paul, 1986.

Crossing the Threshold of Hope. Ed. Vittorio Messori. New York: Alfred A. Knopf, 1994.

Gift and Mystery: On the Fiftieth Anniversary of My Priestly Ordination. New York: Doubleday, 1996.

God, Father and Creator: A Catechesis on the Creed. Vol. 1. Boston: Daughters of St. Paul, 1996.

Jesus, Son and Savior: A Catechesis on the Creed. Vol. 2. Boston: Daughters of St. Paul, 1996.

The thirteen encyclicals issued between 1979 and 1998 may be grouped in the following schema: (1) a Trinitarian trilogy, supplemented by reflection on Christ's work of redemption, (2) a social trilogy, (3) a set on pastoral concerns, and (4) a trilogy on philosophy and moral theology.[5]

A trilogy of encyclicals based on the Holy Trinity has flowed from the Pope's pen in the same order in which the doxology appears in 2 Corinthians 13:14 ("The grace of the Lord Jesus Christ and the love of God and the fellowship of the Holy Spirit be with you all"): *Redemptor Hominis* (1979) on Christ the Redeemer, *Dives in Misericordia* (1980) on the Father of Mercy, and *Dominum et Vivificantem* (1986) on the Holy Spirit. While every one of John Paul's letters is deeply christological, these trinitarian meditations all use the same lens (Christ's work of redemption) that will play into the title of two other encyclicals, *Redemptoris Mater* (1987) and *Redemptoris Missio* (1990). Of these, the former reflects on Mary the Mother of the Redeemer as the first fruit of His work of redemption, and

---

5. The complete text of the encyclicals issued through 1996 along with fine explanatory essays and helpful bibliography is available in *The Encyclicals of John Paul II,* ed. with introductions by J. Michael Miller, C.S.B. (Huntington, Ind.: Our Sunday Visitor, 1996).

the latter concentrates on a theme important throughout his pontificate: the energizing of the Church for her role in the third Christian millennium by a remindfulness of the permanent validity of the Church's missionary vocation in service to the work of the Redeemer.

Early on during his pontificate, John Paul wrote three encyclicals about the Church's social teaching. In each case, the Pope used an anniversary of a previous papal encyclical as an occasion for his own writing, but curiously there is relatively little quotation or reference to the texts of these previous encyclicals. Instead we find additional contributions to the vast anthropological vision of John Paul, ever convinced that only enlightenment by Christ will remedy the perverse displacement of God by faulty visions of man and the many evils confronting contemporary culture as a result of that displacement. In 1981, on the ninetieth anniversary of Leo XIII's *Rerum Novarum,* John Paul issued *Laborem Exercens* (thus following the lead of Pius XI's 1931 *Quadragesimo Anno,* John XXIII's 1961 *Mater et Magistra,* and Paul VI's 1971 *Octagesimo Adveniens*). Ten years later he commemorated the centenary of *Rerum Novarum* with *Centesimus Annus* (1991). In 1987, he issued *Sollicitudo Rei Socialis* on the twentieth anniversary of Paul VI's *Populorum Progressio* (1967). This recurrent concern with anniversaries is not simply sentimental, of course, but seems to be rooted in the Pope's vision that those regions of the world with the deepest historical roots in Christianity are now increasingly exhibiting spiritual impoverishment because they have progressively abandoned those roots. In these encyclicals, the Pope develops what the Church has long been championing as the rights of labor into a profound vision of the solidarity needed to promote human dignity. He also issues a warning about the dangers of liberal capitalism's excesses, balanced by some guidance about the legitimate uses of the free market and other modern economic institutions for the promotion of human culture. Throughout these encyclicals, the Pope repeatedly sounds a theme that is counterintuitive for many modern readers: acknowledging God's sovereignty reveals rather than diminishes human dignity and genuine human freedom. The practical consequences of this vision for society and economics are enormous.

Several of the encyclicals deal with concerns proper to the pastor of the whole Church, including especially *Slavorum Apostoli* and *Ut Unum Sint*. The former (1985) alerts us to the Pope's concern for unity with the Orthodox as well as his mindfulness of the Christian history of the Slavic peoples, a history that began with the missionary efforts of Saints Cyril and Methodius a thousand years ago. The latter (1995) addresses the scandal of continued division within the Church and reminds us of the Gospel-given goal of promoting real unity within the Church. The encyclical *Redemptoris Missio* could also be included under this heading, for it provides the background explanation for the new evangelization (proclaimed in *Euntes in Mundum* and in *Tertio Millennio Adveniente*) as a permanent and ongoing pastoral concern of the Pope for carrying out the mission entrusted to the Church by the Redeemer.

Perhaps the most significant of all the encyclicals is the set devoted to moral theology and, most recently, to the problem of faith and reason. *Veritatis Splendor* (1993) is a treatment, at once biblical and philosophical, of fundamental moral theology, while *Evangelium Vitae* (1995) makes the application of these basic moral truths to some of the most important and controversial issues of our day: abortion, euthanasia, and capital punishment. In the fall of 1998, the Pope issued *Fides et Ratio* as a letter addressed to his fellow bishops on the service of philosophy and theology to the mission of Christ, which is being carried out by the Church. If the social encyclicals show the well-practiced hand of the former archbishop of Krakow in dealing with the Marxists, the moral encyclicals show the skillful teacher of ethics from the Catholic University of Lublin.

In both cases, the Pope devotes an extensive portion of the document to the biblical roots of the Church's teachings on morality (his meditation on the parable of the rich young man in *Veritatis Splendor,* for example, or his reflections on Cain and Abel in *Evangelium Vitae).* What is so important for questions of method in moral theology about the Pope's use of these biblical stories is the way in which he proceeds to draw out from a lengthy phenomenological meditation on these stories the relevant moral lessons and then weaves together a compelling systematic account of the moral teaching of the Church. In doing so, he often uses the traditional categories employed by a Thomistic analysis of moral questions in terms of intention of the moral agent, the nature of the act, and the situation in which an act is done, including the full scope of the consequences of any human action. In this way, the Pope, besides offering us moral insight on important questions of morality, seems to be holding out a model to moral theologians on how to undertake the return to the biblical sources that Vatican Council II called for as a renewal of moral theology and on how to integrate any such efforts in biblical theology into the traditional concerns of Catholic moral theology with natural law theory and the philosophical analysis of the moral act. Although the Pope repeatedly shows his capacities for the work of textual-historical criticism that has marked so much of recent biblical scholarship,[6] he does not exhibit the least paralysis in the use of biblical texts for the development of moral theology.

The encyclical *Fides et Ratio* presents in a new form the Pope's long cherished commitment to the necessary interconnections between philosophy and theology. Here and throughout his works he constantly warns against the perils of pursuing either one without the other. To labor at theol-

---

6. See Terrence Prendergast, S.J., " 'A Vision of Wholeness': A Reflection on the Use of Scripture in a Cross-Section of Papal Writings," in *The Thought of Pope John Paul II: A Collection of Essays and Studies,* ed. John M. McDermott, S.J. (Rome: Gregorian University Press, 1993), 69–92.

ogy without a solid philosophical grounding not only risks fideism[7] but imperils the very human dignity that so much of his own thought has been anxious to defend, as if human reason, especially in the solidarity of the community of human knowers, were unable to gain much purchase on reality. This course could easily leave the way open, in religious matters, to a kind of fundamentalism that shirks the hard work of genuine theological inquiry and, in secular affairs, to the reduction of all authority to mere power,[8] as if there were no objectively discoverable truths of morality to which all — believers and nonbelievers — are bound. On the other hand, to labor at philosophy entirely apart from faith and theological reflection could readily result once again in the desiccations of Enlightenment reason[9] and in the violent reactions that have been provoked under such names as "deconstructionism" and "the postmodern."[10] In virtually all of John Paul's own writings, one can discern the careful interweaving of various philosophical methods and his own distinctive style of theological reflection, so it is no surprise to find in the new encyclical his defense of the interplay of faith and reason as a kind of "circle" — but one designed to be mutually fruitful rather than vicious.[11]

Some Recurrent Themes: Christology, the Relation of Truth to Freedom and Conscience, and the Theology of the Body

There are three topics that the Pope has recurrently treated: the anthropological Christology of his encyclicals; the relation of truth, freedom, and conscience in his ethical writings, including the encyclical *Veritatis Splendor;* and the

---

7. *Fides et Ratio,* nos. 48 and 52.
8. *Redemptor Hominis,* no. 17.
9. *Fides et Ratio,* no. 51.
10. Ibid., no. 91.
11. Ibid., nos. 73 and 100.

theology of the body, found especially in his catechetical works.

Christ, the Redeemer of Man

From the time of his first encyclical in 1979, *Redemptor Hominis,* the Pope has repeatedly sounded a theme that he clearly considers to be of the greatest urgency. He sees the world as suffering from a profound crisis of dehumanization, and he sees the Church as having a divinely commissioned vocation to speak out for the intrinsic dignity of the human person in the face of all opposition. For the Church, this task is a participation in the mission of Christ the Redeemer.

The practical applications of this insight have stretched from guiding the challenge that has been mounted against Eastern Europe's totalitarian regimes, through reminding the free societies of the West not to squander their heritage on godless pleasures, to organizing international alliances in concert with many Islamic and Latin delegations at various United Nations conferences (such as Cairo, Beijing, and Rome) for the protection of human life and of the family.

These high-level efforts seem to be linked fundamentally to the new evangelization to which he has repeatedly summoned the whole Church. Historically, the period of evangelization that just preceded our own began with the waves of missionaries that were sent in the sixteenth century to newly discovered lands, which continued with virtually the same élan until about a generation ago. The new evangelization of the Pope proceeds not only by inspiring peoples who are not Christian with a vision of the dignity afforded humanity by divine love in the person of Christ but also by reminding peoples who at some point in their national life have accepted Christianity as their true history,[12] whether it be a Western nation that now hazards the loss of its soul in

---

12. See, for example, *Redemptor Hominis,* no. 16, on "the true culture of peoples."

the chase after material prosperity or some poorer nation just emerging from totalitarian domination. One need only think of the contrast between, on the one hand, the lively papal speeches in Cuba in January 1998 about the authentic heritage of the Cuban people over the five centuries since the arrival of Christianity and their formation as a people and, on the other hand, Castro's dreary speeches about Cubans as the pitiable victims of oppression by others. Even the Pope's relative silence about the regime of the last forty years seems to be part of this strategy, as if the recent dictatorship is but a sad blip on the radar screen that he could dismiss with just a few pointed remarks compared to the authentic and dignified history of this people and to the exciting possibilities for their future.

Redemptor Hominis presents not so much a treatise on Christology as an account of the significance for humanity of the mystery of redemption in Christ. As a sacramental sign of our union with God, the Church has the mission[13] tirelessly to point out that the direction one must take is toward Christ the Redeemer: there is no salvation anywhere else. The redemption is a new creation, a restoration of what sin has damaged by all sorts of violence and deceit. By reason of Christ's full humanity in every respect but sin, Christ "fully reveals man to himself." By reason of His divinity, Christ alone can reconcile us with the Father. For John Paul, it is the yoking of these human and divine dimensions of the mystery of redemption that generates "authentic humanism," a religion marked by adoration of the one true God and by deep wonder at man himself, the very image of God.

Again and again in these encyclicals, one finds the Pope concentrating on the theme of truth and freedom in much the way he enunciates it in *Redemptor Hominis,* 12: earnest pursuit of truth and deep respect for it once discovered are indispensable conditions for authentic human freedom. Just as in the second chapter of *Veritatis Splendor,* the

---

13. Ibid., no. 11.

Pope distinguishes between true and false freedom so as
not to confuse what normally gets bruited about as freedom (whether as some idea about unconstrained liberty to
do entirely as one pleases, or as the popular notion that in
our freedom we can simply *decide* what is true rather than
having to *discover* it) with the authentic idea of freedom
implied by a passage such as John 8:32 ("the truth will
set you free"). Invoking *Dignitatis Humanae* (Vatican II's
Declaration on Religious Freedom — a document that has
received fairly universal praise, except from the Traditional-
ist movement), John Paul insists that the truth that has been
revealed to us by God imposes on us the obligation to guard
and teach this truth as a divine gift. Those ideas of freedom
that fail to embrace "the whole truth about man," including the awareness of absolute norms for the conscience, the
inviolability of human dignity, and the human capacity to
discover and respect truths that have been discovered, can
readily lead to the substitution of empty surrogates in its
place. In practice, freedom's misuse is likely to prevent a
person from gaining even what Augustine called "the be-
ginnings of freedom, the freedom from crime," let alone
any growth of the person in mature freedom.

The Problem of Conscience in Veritatis Splendor

There are many places in these encyclicals where the Pope
makes particularly telling use of philosophy to advance his
case. The passage on conscience and truth from the second
chapter of *Veritatis Splendor* (*VS*) offers a good example
to illustrate this theme. The Pope argues that certain trends
in current theology fail to respect the intrinsic link between
freedom and truth (especially the tendency to exalt freedom
to the status of an absolute, as if it were the source of all
values, rather than to stress that the perfection of freedom
consists in choosing to live in the truth about what is good
for human beings); he then turns to the topic of conscience.

John Paul undertakes to praise what he can about recent philosophical and theological developments before

undertaking to criticize what he considers defective and to make his own contribution to the question. He praises the "heightened sense...of the respect due to the journey of conscience" toward truth as one of the authentic achievements of modern culture. But mindful that there is also a widespread cultural trend toward setting the freedom of conscience up against the Church's teachings on morality, he argues that a mistaken idea of conscience is the source of a dangerous error, namely, treating an individual's conscience as if it were the source of truth and value and thus an infallible sort of court that precludes appeal to any other authority. Those who maintain such a position tend to presume that conscience generates autonomous "decisions" and to claim that those with maturity in making such decisions are not liable for obedience to the moral law or to any truth higher than themselves. But this would be to set freedom and law into an antagonism likely to result in subjective relativism by treating the final decision about what is good and what is evil simply as a decision made by the individual conscience. This would be to ignore what the moral law teaches to be intrinsically evil by allowing an individual to do with a clear conscience what is intrinsically evil.

The Pope's argumentation on this problem involves both supple phenomenological investigation of conscience and sturdy Thomistic distinctions.[14] Conscience, he reminds us, names those acts of practical reason that use objective norms by which an individual comes to know what one may or may not do. The judgment of conscience is not a "creative" decision-maker that can create the good, but an application of the moral law to a particular case, and thus "the witness of God himself, whose voice and judgment penetrates the depths of man's soul."[15] It is divine law that constitutes the universal and objective norm of moral-

---

14. For a thorough analysis of the ethical argumentation in *Veritatis Splendor,* see Alasdair MacIntyre, "How Can We Learn What *Veritatis Splendor* Has to Teach?" in *The Thomist* 58 (1994): 171–95.

15. *VS,* no. 58.

ity. What any moral agent needs to supply for making true judgments of conscience is a "heart converted to the Lord and to the love of what is good."[16]

The Pope then delivers a short catechism on the obligations of Christians to form their consciences in light of the Church's teachings, for he is mindful here as always that cultural and historical currents vary and that the first principles of practical reason, which are infallibly imprinted on the conscience of every person, need to be extended to more specific principles. It is both a matter of having effective mediating structures like family and parishes to work at the ongoing formation of conscience and a matter of recognizing our constant need for divine mercy by asking for forgiveness when we are confronted with our bad conscience out of a sense of any disproportion between the demands of the moral law and our readiness to fulfill them.

The philosophical support for assertions like these comes in two crucial sections on natural law and on the moral act. Working from a solidly Thomistic understanding of the natural law as "the participation of the practical reason in the wisdom of the divine Creator and Lawgiver,"[17] John Paul argues that the Creator, the author of human nature, has written the light of reason into the heart of every person, and it is by the light of the natural law that people can discover what they need to do and what they need to avoid. As before, he feels the need to critique several current trends in philosophy and theology that are obscuring this proper understanding of natural law. First, some moralists claim that "norms" are only established by statistical study of concrete human behavior patterns and the opinions about morality encountered in the majority of people."[18] To this the Pope responds that statistics do not reveal to us what anyone should do but only what people on the average actually do. As such, they are as likely to give us information

16. Ibid., no. 64.
17. Ibid., no. 40.
18. Ibid., no. 46.

about what the norm is designed to curb as about what the norm requires.

Second, to those who oppose natural law because of its alleged physicalism, and who claim that people are at liberty to handle nature in any way they like (arguing, for instance, that human nature is the source of all sorts of artificial inventions that improve life by taking care of unfortunate consequences), John Paul II retorts that such a position overlooks the moral significance of the body's natural inclinations and, in effect, reduces "the human person to a 'spiritual' and purely formal freedom."[19] Not only is such a theory excessively abstract, but it is forgetful of a deep and important insight about the real unity of the human person, a unity of body and soul that requires ethics to be as reverent to the body as to the soul.

Third, the Pope counters those whose sensitivity to the way that all knowledge is conditioned by culture and history leads them to deny the universality and immutability of the norms of natural law. To this end, the Pope appeals to the transcendental nature of the human person as the measure of any culture in which one finds oneself. Granting a legitimate realm for cultures to find specific applications of natural law, the Pope insists that natural law is the law God made for the good of human beings as such. For this reason, its negative precepts (for example, the prohibition on taking the life of the innocent) "are universally valid" and oblige "always and under all circumstances."[20] The natural law can come to be known to any one "endowed with reason and living in history," and "it is precisely on the path of the moral life that the way of salvation is open to all."

A companion section on "the moral act" is also a part of the Pope's philosophical arsenal in this chapter. We find not only a resiliently Thomistic analysis of the moral act but also a profound engagement with several prominent

---

19. Ibid., no. 49.
20. Ibid., no. 52.

ethical theories that he opposes: consequentialism and pro-portionalism. The general point of consequentialism is the view that a specific act can only be regarded as moral or immoral once its likely consequences have been evaluated. Proportionalists tend to include a broader sweep of consid-erations in the moral judgments a person renders about an act, with special concentration on the proportionality of the good and bad effects of any choice (including evaluation of "the lesser evil" as well as "the greater good"). But both schools of moral analysis maintain that the ethical evalua-tion of an act should take place by sizing up the positive and negative values that will result from the act in order to choose a course of action whose anticipated effects will be the most positive (or least negative).

What the Pope objects to here (following Romans 3:8) is the attempt in both schools of thought to justify an intrin-sically evil act, that is, the acceptance of the position that one may do evil so that good may come. Agreeing that a person must include consideration of intention and conse-quences in any moral evaluation, the Pope also insists that the crux of moral analysis is consideration of the object that one is freely choosing: "The morality of the human act depends principally and fundamentally on the 'object' natu-rally chosen by the deliberate will." The object of one's free choice is what primarily determines whether a given act "is capable of being ordered to the good and to the ultimate end, which is God."[21] But since certain kinds of action are not able to be ordered to God, they must be acknowledged to be intrinsically evil. That is, "they radically contradict the good of the person made in His image" and so they can never be acceptable, whatever good intention or anticipated consequences one brings to bear. The list of examples the Pope then quotes from *Gaudium et Spes*, no. 27, is telling:

> What is hostile to life itself, such as any kind of homi-
> cide, genocide, abortion, euthanasia, and voluntary

---

21. Ibid., nos. 78–79.

suicide; whatever violates the integrity of the human person, such as mutilation, physical and mental torture, and attempts to coerce the spirit; whatever is offensive to human dignity, such as subhuman living conditions, arbitrary imprisonment, deportation, slavery, prostitution, and trafficking in women and children; degrading conditions of work which treat laborers as mere instruments of profit and not as free responsible persons: all these and the like are a disgrace, and so long as they infect human civilization they contaminate those who inflict them more than those who suffer injustice, and they are a negation of the honor due to the Creator. (*VS*, no. 80)

In short, the Pope reaffirms the traditional Catholic position on morality, that even for the most noble of motives one may never do evil that good may come.

The Theology of the Body

Catechesis, the instruction of the faithful, has been as central a concern for this Pope as has been the effort to make a genuine contribution to the state of the question in the area of freedom, morality, and conscience. Within the list of his writings, we find a series of catechetical lectures, now collected into various small volumes, including: *Original Unity of Man and Woman: Catechesis on the Book of Genesis; Blessed are the Pure of Heart: Catechesis on the Sermon on the Mount and Writings of St. Paul; Reflections on Humanae Vitae: Conjugal Morality and Spirituality; The Theology of Marriage and Celibacy: Catechesis on Marriage and Celibacy; A Catechesis on the Creed: God, Father and Creator* and *Jesus, Son and Savior.* Although delivered in serial form to enormous general audiences, these lectures have been brought together into short books that exhibit the mind of the teacher that Karol Wojtyla was long before he became Pope John Paul II. By way of example, let us consider here just one of the important themes, the theology of the body presented in sixty-three Wednesday audiences between September 5, 1979, and May 6, 1981, as the papal exposition of a theme that he began to work out in earlier books such as *Love and Responsibility* (1960).

Commenting on the pair of biblical accounts about the creation of Adam and Eve in Genesis, the Pope develops his views on the specifically Christian meaning of human embodiment and on the role of the human body and of all our physical acts for the expression of the person that each human being is.[22] In other words, just as the deliberate, conscious acts of any person (proceeding from such interior structures of the person as the mind and the will) are designed by the Creator and are supposed to be used in such a way that they reflect the goodness of our Creator, so too all the exterior structures of the body have been designed by the same Creator and have been placed under the control of human reason so that they too can express the individual person and so that they too can reflect the goodness of the Creator. Far from any "fear of the flesh," a charge that has sometimes been laid against Christianity despite its doctrine of the resurrection of the body and the long history of repudiating any form of Manicheanism,[23] the Pope treats the human body as always deserving a special reverence precisely because Genesis describes it as the gift of the Creator just as much as the human soul (with which it forms the integrated unity that is the human person).

Not only is embodied existence a gift which an individual person receives from God, but there is a meaning embedded in this embodiment that is crucial to the human vocation of self-giving. By tracing the three "original human experiences" of solitude, original unity, and nakedness, whose

---

22. There is a fine treatment of this subject in Richard M. Hogan and John M. LeVoir, *Covenant of Love: Pope John Paul II on Sexuality, Marriage, and Family in the Modern World* (New York: Doubleday, 1985; San Francisco: Ignatius Press, 1992), 39–70.

23. One need only think of Augustine's repudiation of the error of Manicheanism (to which he had earlier been attracted) in his *Confessions*, or of the spiritual battles waged by the Dominicans against its medieval version as Albigensianism.

descriptions in Genesis the Pope takes to be valid for everyone precisely by virtue of the fact that we are all (like Adam) made in God's image, he proposes a theology of the body in which the "meaning" that resides in the body can be "communicated" in the relationships into which the person chooses to enter. This meaning will either be communicated authentically by the gift of oneself to another in a freely chosen and rightly ordered commitment, or communicated inauthentically in some form of domination or some purely utilitarian employment of human bodies that fails to respect the fact that the body is always an expression of the person and thus already has "a meaning" intended by the Creator. In short, one can speak the truth or tell a lie about love with the use of one's body just as with the use of one's voice. Telling the truth is both a matter of saying with one's body what one actually intends in one's mind and a matter of saying (with mind and body) what one is able to say and should say, given one's situation and readiness for commitment. Giving one's body to someone other than one's spouse, for example, is a kind of lie, for the adulterer is, in effect, saying that the new partner may use what in justice belongs to someone else. Likewise, those engaging in premarital sex are offering to the other a gift of the self that neither is yet ready fully to give.

The Pope's method of arguing toward these conclusions in *Blessed Are the Pure of Heart* and *Reflections on Humanae Vitae* proceeds by a prolonged study of Genesis in *Original Unity of Man and Woman*. In Adam's solitude at the very beginning of creation, the Pope finds an agonizing loneliness that provokes the discovery that Adam, while still alone, could not fulfill himself in the way God intended. Created in the image of God, Adam is made to do what God does, that is, to love. But to do so he needs to express his love for someone in the way that God has made him, that is, as a person with a body, which expresses that person. Only when Adam comes fully to feel the loneliness of his solitude can he adequately relish the gift of another human being.

Reflecting on the spiritual and physical joy that Adam and Eve must have experienced for one another when Adam "awoke" from the sleep during which God took from him a rib to make Eve, the Pope finds in the original unity of the love between these persons a biblical testimony to "the nuptial meaning" of the body, understood in terms of the complementarity of male and female.[24] God intended for the unity of their love to be realized in a bodily way, for bodies are crucial to the expression of the person, and sexuality is what makes possible the physical union that is a bodily means of expressing a loving gift of self to the other. Noting that a human body not governed by the faculties of intellect and will would no longer be capable of expressing the person, the Pope can distinguish between "authentic" and "inauthentic" uses of the body (one's own or that of another), such that the meaning which a body possesses for the expression of the person can truthfully reflect the dignity of the person, or fail to do so by falsifying that meaning in a variety of ways.[25]

In their original nakedness, Adam and Eve felt none of the shame that came later with sin. The Pope envisions Adam and Eve as fully conscious of the "meaning" of their bodies and the opportunity to express through their bodies the kind of love that God intended them to share with one another as the persons whom He had made, Adam and Eve. But the integrity that they experienced was shattered by original sin, one of whose consequences for all of us who have come afterward is the inevitability of some inner struggle between the desires of the flesh and what we come to understand as the right order of love and commitment. The temptation that Satan manufactured for Eve, after all,

---

24. See especially the lecture of January 9, 1980, in *Original Unity,* 106–12.

25. In the course of this elaboration of a biblical theology of the body we find again and again a very direct and appealing way of articulating the same insights that are expressed in the far more technical language of philosophy in *Love and Responsibility,* especially chaps. 2 and 3 on the differences between emotional and sensual urges and the ways in which the range of bodily and psychic reactions to "the other" need to be incorporated into truly human love.

did not concern the luscious nature of the fruit (an appeal to her appetites, which at that point were not yet out of harmony with her intellect), but an appeal directly to the intellect and will, the idea that she could have knowledge by which to decide what is good and what is evil, a power which God reserved to Himself. Through the sin of pride, Adam and Eve lost the gift of integration between mind and body that they had enjoyed, and so their desire to control the world by having an equality with God results in the lack of any easy control over their own bodies.

For John Paul, this is an important aspect of the discovery of their nakedness and the experience of shame: their bodies no longer perfectly expressed their persons. In lust they began to seek one another as a way to gratify themselves rather than using their bodies as a means of mutual self-donation. They experienced shame not so much over their own bodies but over the very strength of the desires they felt to use one another and over their weakness at directing themselves to the proper use of their bodies, even though they genuinely wanted to do the right thing. Although now driven by lusts of various types, men and women can still find the strength to make their bodies an appropriate expression of the persons they are meant to be by committed love, by the "sincere giving" of self to other in the commitment of marriage. By contrast, all the other forms of using sexuality amount to some form of self-gratification, whether the selling of bodies in pornography and prostitution, the self-manipulation of masturbation, the treatment of the body as some kind of manipulable machine in the case of vasectomies or contraception, or even the mutual permission of consenting but unmarried adults to use another for pleasure or as a remedy for the loneliness of an individual's solitude.

Working out in detail such applications for the theology of the body that the Pope finds latent in such texts as Genesis has become the task for many of his subsequent catechetical lectures. The 1986 volume entitled *The Theol-*

*ogy of Marriage and Celibacy: Catechesis on Marriage and
Celibacy* attempts some of this work. But equally important lessons are also available in many of the Pope's plays.
The most famous of his dramatic works is *The Jeweler's
Shop*,[26] a story in three acts about the nature of the commitment that is marriage and the contingencies that are the
context for living out the promises that we make. The action of the play takes place in front of a jeweler's shop, first
in the conversation of a young couple flushed with love and
readying themselves for marriage. The action then turns to a
second couple whose marriage is on the rocks, with both of
the spouses blaming the other but unable for the most part
to see even a mote of responsibility in their own eyes. Only
when the woman tries to sell back her ring and the jeweler
informs her that one ring alone weighs nothing does she
come to any sense of her own culpability for what has gone
wrong. In the third act we find the son from the first marriage and the daughter from the second, deeply in love and
anxious to marry but mindful of the troubles that life may
bring. She is mindful that her parents once loved each other
very much, but now they only fight; his mother, we learn,
had raised him alone after his father was killed in the war.
Much as in the catechetical lectures written as Pope, this
early play by the young priest Karol Wojtyla is profoundly
alert to the ways in which the choices of our wills and the
actions of our bodies express the persons that we are.

Conclusion

There is much more one could say about so prolific a Pope,
but perhaps what we have covered here will be of some
use for studying his thought. One should follow the voice
that inspired Augustine at the time of his conversion: *tolle et
lege* — take it up and read it! It will prove extremely helpful

---

26. Contained in *The Collected Plays and Writings on Theater* along with many
other interesting pieces. See especially *The Radiance of Fatherhood* for some of
his thoughts on the relation of human fatherhood to its divine prototype.

to read with pen in hand, jotting down a quick summary or paraphrase as one reads along. By doing so, one will be much in the spirit of a Pontiff who has generated so many words, for his work is designed to evoke our own words and to assist our efforts in appreciating the truth about man that Christ came to reveal. From the theater of the word that Wojtyla's early dramatic groups were trying to stage through the learned discussions his encyclicals promote, John Paul's thought has aimed at handing down faithfully a message he has received and devising new ways to make such perennial truths fresh and attractive.

Chapter 2

John Paul II's Seminal Contributions to Moral Theology

Foundational Issues

WILLIAM B. SMITH

Pope John Paul II has had the longest pontificate of the twentieth century, and the doctrinal-moral patrimony of this Pope, while not yet complete, is now quite extensive — indeed, very extensive. His pastoral papal teaching, moreover, is remarkable for the continuity and consistency with his immediate predecessors and with the central ecclesial event of this century — Vatican Council II.

A case can be made that most of the moral teaching of Vatican Council II is, in large part, the moral teaching of Pius XII. In a biographical entry in the *New Catholic Encyclopedia,* one author writing of Pope Pius XII points out that the volume and scope of his teaching "surpassed any of his predecessors." Furthermore, the moral teaching of the *Catechism of the Catholic Church* (1992) is deeply indebted to the same Vatican Council along with its faithful exposition by Paul VI and even more so by John Paul II. Yet it is fair to say that the doctrinal-moral patrimony of John Paul II has surpassed the scope and volume of even that of Pius XII and will have the same influence in the twenty-first century as Pius XII had on the twentieth. Karol

---

MSGR. WILLIAM B. SMITH, S.T.D., is Professor of Moral Theology at St. Joseph's Seminary, Yonkers, New York.

Wojtyla was nineteen years old when Pius XII assumed the papacy in 1939. The philosophical and theological education he received during his ecclesiastical training and seminary eduction was dominated by the "school" of Pius XII. His pontificate began in 1978, immediately after the miniature reign of John Paul I, but more significantly, after the fifteen-year pontificate of Paul VI.

John Paul II has often referred to Paul VI as his "spiritual father." It was Paul VI who presided over and directed three of the four sessions of Vatican II (1963–65), and the same Paul VI who directed the immediate implementation of that Council. John Paul, as Cardinal Karol Wojtyla, archbishop of Krakow, was an active and attentive bishop participant in every session of the Council — from its opening to its closing day. Aware of and explicit about the need to interpret the Council correctly and to defend it against what he calls "tendentious interpretations," John Paul II is the most faithful expositor, even champion, of the true teaching of Vatican Council II.

There are some faddists who, either ignorant of or antagonistic to the Council's true teaching, popularize the deceit that this Pope and the current prefect of the Congregation for the Doctrine of the Faith, Cardinal Joseph Ratzinger, are trying, somehow, to reverse the Council. Some of these critics are so blinded by personal ideologies or agendas that they argue that the Pope is trying today to restore "minority" positions set aside at the Council and thereby replace the "majority" positions actually taught by the Council. This distorted claim — sometimes fostered by a complicit media — could not be further from the truth. In his apostolic letter *Tertio Millennio Adveniente* (1994), John Paul teaches that the best preparation for the new millennium can "only be expressed in a renewed commitment to apply, as faithfully as possible, the teachings of Vatican II to the life of every individual and of the whole Church" (no. 20).

And so, as the initial phase of individual and ecclesial

preparation for the new millennium, John Paul proposes a serious "examination of conscience."

The Pope's moral masterpiece on fundamental moral theology is his encyclical *Veritatis Splendor,* published in 1993. He writes:

> The specific purpose of the present encyclical is this: to set forth, with regard to the problems being discussed, the principles of a moral teaching based on Sacred Scripture and the living Apostolic Tradition, and at the same time to shed light on the presuppositions and consequences of the dissent which that teaching has met. (no. 5)

The previous year the *Catechism of the Catholic Church* (1992) was published. Although John Paul gives generous credit to Cardinal Joseph Ratzinger for the publication of the *Catechism,* the Holy Father views the *Catechism* as indispensable "in order that all the richness of the teaching of the Church following the Second Vatican Council could be preserved in a new synthesis and be given a new direction." While not explicitly called for by the Council, the *Catechism* completes the teaching implementation of Vatican Council II.

Part III of the *Catechism* ("Life in Christ") is the moral part of the *Catechism.* Part III is divided into two sections. The first section concerns fundamental moral theology (nos. 1691–2051), while the second section treats specific moral questions (nos. 2052–57). Even the inclusions in this part of the *Catechism* are instructive, for example, "Person and Society" (nos. 1877–96); "Participation in Social Life" (nos. 1897–1927); and "Social Justice" (nos. 1928–48). What in the past have been thought of as social justice issues are now included and taught as part of the fundamental moral theology of the Catholic Church.

Conventional Catholic moral teaching was for some time seen as almost indistinguishable from canonical discipline. In many seminaries, both subjects were taught by the same teacher. During his pontificate, John Paul has overseen the promulgation of a new Code of Canon Law for the Western Church — *Codex Iuris Canonici* (1983). Also, for the first time in history, a complete codification of the canon law of the Eastern churches has been promulgated — *Codex Canonum Ecclesiarum Orientalium* (1990). This legal renewal fulfilled the request and mandate of the Fathers of Vatican Council II. It is thus all the more remarkable that amid this canonical achievement, John Paul II did not leave moral theology as an adjunct of canon law, but renewed it by returning to the "sacred sources" of sacred theology, especially Sacred Scripture.

In moral teaching, John Paul has made contributions to four foundational issues: (1) moral methodology; (2) christological basis; (3) moral epistemology; and (4) personalist morality.

Moral Methodology and the Sacred Sources

The sacred sources of theology are Sacred Scripture (revealed by God); Sacred Tradition (guided by the Holy Spirit); and the Magisterium of the Church (which enjoys a charism given it by Jesus Christ to teach in His name). Since moral theology is part of sacred theology, it has the same sacred sources, yet since at least from the beginning of the seventeenth century, moral theology as a discipline was taught and treated as a separate science. Over time, this had the unfortunate perceived effect of seeming to separate moral doctrine from its sacred sources. Consequently, Catholic moral teaching seemed to have less and less to do with principles located in Sacred Scripture than with legal and canonical authorities as well as so-called approved authors. The net effect was that our moral teaching seemed to have only remote connections with Divine Revelation and to be more connected with juridic casuistry.

This fostered the perception that morality was largely a morality of obligation, especially a morality of external obligation. For many, the whole science of morality was seemingly external to them and largely a matter of law — of whatever kind: natural, divine, canonical, or civil. Everything was a question of liberty or law, or liberty from law. For many, morality was seen as a negative avoidance: How far can I go before I fall off? How far can I go before I commit formal sin? What is the least or best I can do to fulfill some law without actually violating it?

This minimalist mentality and casuistry became oppressive and distorted. The Gospel and the key place of virtue and the virtues in Thomistic ethics simply faded out of moral theology and landed, if anywhere, in ascetics or spiritual theology. Moral theology was taught as if the rich biblical and patristic themes, along with the doctrinal presuppositions, were separate from it and not really relevant to it.

The methodological contribution of John Paul to Catholic moral theology is a fundamental correction to this aberration. In all of his major moral teachings, he always begins, not with a canon or a philosopher, but with a reflection on biblically revealed principles. Consider perhaps the two best known examples: *Veritatis Splendor* begins with a careful and detailed meditation on Matthew 19, the dialogue with the rich young man; and *Evangelium Vitae* (1995) begins with an extended reflection on Genesis 4, the Cain and Able passages. This is not just a personal style of writing; it is an important methodological starting point for moral theology — Sacred Scripture. The Pope is emphatic that sound morals rest on sound doctrine; the life of faith and the moral life cannot be separated (see *Veritatis Splendor,* no. 4).

"Teacher, what *good* must I do to gain eternal life?" (Matt. 19:16). Jesus answers: "If you wish to enter into life, keep the commandments." That answer will surprise no Christian. What might surprise some readers is that so many Christian authors find no real content, no concrete moral direction in this authoritative answer. The Pope, by contrast, weaves this biblical text throughout his encyclical on the truth about the good (*Veritatis Splendor,* nos. 6–17).

Some moral revisionists, on the other hand, have emptied the moral content of Revelation by arguing that it is too time-bound, that it says nothing that reaches or binds our time, or, at best, that Sacred Scripture offers only general orientations, invitations, advice, or as the academic jargon has it, *parenesis,* that is, exhortation.

Even more radical is the position of W. C. Spohn, writing about the Magisterium and morality in *Theological Studies* (March 1993), where he says bluntly:

> Morality, however, does not belong to the Church because it does not rest on revelation;... Faith comes from hearing the gospel, while morals come from hearing a much wider chorus of voices. (106)

"Morality... does not rest on revelation." That is an amazing statement that simply reduces the content of Divine Revelation to a minor key or perhaps just background music. Whereas, the whole first chapter of *Veritatis Splendor* culminates and concludes with a strong repudiation of theories and methodologies that separate and/or evacuate moral content from biblical revelation (nos. 25–27).

The call and challenge of Vatican Council II to renew moral theology by renewed contact with sacred sources and show the nobility of the Christian vocation to virtue were not really answered by professional moralists. After the Council, at least in the English-speaking world, moral theology was paralyzed by two bitter and lasting debates: debates about artificial birth control and about divorce and remarriage, wherein the secular media played a bigger role than did the sacred sources of theology.

The Pope, however, has led the way in responding faithfully to the challenge of the Council precisely by recovering the biblical, patristic, and magisterial sources as the methodological starting point of his major moral documents and moral teaching. This also has a genuine ecumenical thrust — a point more often appreciated by Evangelical authors than by some Catholic ones.

Christological Basis and Focus

The second seminal contribution to Catholic moral teaching of John Paul is the pervasive christological emphasis in his teaching. John Paul is a man transparently in love with Jesus Christ — the center of his preaching and teaching and of his thinking and living.

In his first encyclical, *Redemptor Hominis* (1979), John Paul reminds us that truth is not a principle but a person — Jesus Christ, the Redeemer of man. In his popular book *Crossing the Threshold of Hope* (1994), the Pope writes passionately:

> Christ is absolutely original and absolutely unique. . . .
> He is the one mediator between God and humanity.
> Mediator because He is both God and Man. . . . One
> must never tire of repeating this. Despite some common aspects, Christ does not resemble Mohammed,
> Socrates, or Buddha. He is totally original and unique!
> (42–45).

Referring to *Gaudium et Spes* of Vatican Council II, he writes: "The truth is that only in the mystery of the Incarnate Word does the mystery of man take on light" (no. 22). Jesus Christ is the living truth about God and about man. In other words, one cannot understand the human person, or even oneself, unless one knows something about Jesus Christ.

Another christological teaching of the Council that pervades the teaching of John Paul is found in *Gaudium et Spes*, no. 24, concerning the nature of our human vocation. Speaking of a certain likeness between the union of the Divine Persons and the union of the children of God in truth and charity, the Council teaches: "This likeness reveals that man, who is the only creature on earth which God willed for itself, cannot fully find himself except through a sincere gift of himself (Luke 17:33)."

One can only fully find (fulfill) himself through a sincere gift of self. The Holy Father cites this passage of *Gaudium et Spes* more often than any other teaching of the Council in all his teaching — formal or informal. This single text is the key to a correct understanding of Christian personalism and a needed antidote to resist the mistaken notion of freedom that fuels unqualified secular individualism.

Our human journey, our moral journey must be a free one, or it is not worthy of the name human or moral. Christian personalism sees no personal degradation in status when we freely are obedient to the truth; rather, such obedience is the peculiar expression of human dignity, the ability to discern and to respond to genuine values. In his book *The Acting Person* (1981), he writes: "The person realizes himself most adequately in the fulfillment of his obligations." The same point is repeated frequently throughout his book *Love and Responsibility* (1981) and in his *Letter to Families* (1994).

Giving of self is the essence of Christian personalism; it is only through a sincere gift of self that one can find or fulfill oneself. "Whoever seeks to preserve his life will lose it, but whoever loses it will save it" (Luke 17:33). That is not only the teaching of Jesus, but the very expression of his life. This is a foundational issue for moral theology because it teaches not only what to live but how to live it. It is only through a sincere gift of self that any one of us can live the nobility of the Christian vocation of the faithful and our obligation to bring forth fruit in charity for the life of the world.

Moral Epistemology: The Truth about the Good

The third contribution to Catholic moral theology of John Paul is his attention to moral epistemology, especially evident and developed in the encyclical *Veritatis Splendor* (1993). To my knowledge, no prior moral document of the

Magisterium compares with this. The encyclical consists of an Introduction (nos. 1–5) and three chapters: on biblical foundations (nos. 6–27), on moral reasoning, sound and unsound (nos. 28–83), and on pastoral directives (nos. 84–120). The connections with the *Catechism of the Catholic Church* (1992) are both obvious and explicit throughout. One cannot accept one without the other because *Veritatis Splendor* is the fundamental moral and theological underpinning of the general and specific moral teaching of the *Catechism*.

The encyclical does not shrink from addressing and critiquing almost every post–Vatican Council II moral virus that has infected or afflicted the Church. Healthy trends of concord and cohesion are confirmed and encouraged; all theories of division and dissent are repudiated.

Veritatis Splendor unashamedly lives up to its name: it is very much about truth. Apart from teaching the truth, one central theme is the place and importance of moral epistemology — if there is no truth to be known, there is no truth to be lived. Over and over, the Pope anchors all moral questions on the truth: freedom, law, conscience, goodness, human acts, moral acts, witness, and even the ultimate witness, martyrdom — all are centered on, rooted in and dependent upon truth.

Pragmatists might ask: "What good is truth?" Believers can ask: "What's true about the good?" *Veritatis Splendor* addresses these questions at some length and in much detail. As mentioned above, the Pope begins with the biblical question: "Teacher, what *good* must I do to gain eternal life?" (Matt. 19:16), and he weaves this biblical text throughout his encyclical on the truth about the good.

Focused on the truth, *Veritatis Splendor* is not directed at reconstructed or deconstructed trends; the real target is moral relativism — the acid rain that erodes all moral standards, personal and social. For centuries, the Judeo-Christian ethic served as the foundation of our personal and social standards. It was, once, functionally the "objective moral order" that all citizens presumed or appealed to, including the higher background of our civil law. For some time now, that Judeo-Christian ethic has looked more like a receding hairline than the higher background of our personal and social life. It is not without reason that the Pope so vigorously repudiates theories that uncouple moral teachings from their Old and New Testament roots.

The encyclical presupposes and argues throughout for the existence of an "objective moral order." The second and longest part (nos. 28–82) addresses the questions crucial to fundamental moral theology: freedom and truth; conscience and truth. For some, freedom and law do not belong in the same sentence, yet their claims for absolute autonomy of the "sovereign self" are not rooted in revelation nor compatible with it. True freedom is the freedom to detect or discover the truth, not to invent truth. If there is no norm or standard, no rule or truth outside myself, then all that's left is autonomy (self-norm), and that is moral relativism.

But such radical individualism is not the engine that drives the Judeo-Christian ethic. The same radically false autonomy precludes any normative understanding of natural moral law (nos. 42–45). The light of reason is the light of discerning good from evil, discerning "an imprint on us of the divine light" (no. 42); it is not just staring fixedly at a mirror.

Conscience discovers the truth, detects the truth; conscience does not invent the truth. Conscience is not the right to my own self-will. Quite the contrary, as the great Cardinal John Henry Newman noted in a letter to the duke of Norfolk: "that is a counterfeit of conscience which eighteen prior centuries never heard of and could not mistake for the original."

The connection between conscience and the truth is crucial. In his encyclical *Fides et Ratio* (1998), John Paul outlines some "Current Tasks for Theology" (nos. 92–99). Above all, theology "must look to the ultimate truth which revelation entrusts to it ... so that the truth may once again be known and expressed" (no. 92).

The negative consequences of poor or absent epistemology apply equally to moral theology. As John Paul points out:

> In the Encyclical Letter *Veritatis Splendor,* I wrote that many of the problems of the contemporary world stem from a crisis of truth. I noted that "once the idea of a universal truth about the good, knowable by human reason, is lost, inevitably the notion of conscience also changes. Conscience is no longer considered in its prime reality as an act of a person's intelligence, the function of which is to apply the universal knowledge of the good in a specific situation and thus to express a judgment about the right conduct to be chosen here and now. Instead, there is a tendency to grant to the individual conscience the prerogative of independently determining the criteria of good and evil and then act accordingly. Such an outlook is quite congenial to an individualistic ethic, wherein each individual is faced with his own truth different from the truth of others." (no. 98)

It is both revealing and instructive that John Paul's insistence on moral epistemology — the truth about the good; and the truth about the human person — is a consistent theme throughout his pontificate.

The final part of Chapter II of *Veritatis Splendor* concerns specific acts (nos. 65–70) and the correct understanding of the moral act (nos. 71–83) with an emphasis on what are called "exceptionless norms" or "intrinsic evils." These are specific concrete acts that are never choice-worthy in the Catholic perspective because they never promote the true good of the human person nor the true good of the human community. It is here that John Paul repudiates all false body-soul dualisms (nos. 45–50), as well as trendy "fundamental option" theories (nos. 69–70) and specifically condemns as "false solutions" the revisionist theories called "consequentialism" and "proportionalism" in moral theology (no. 75). The Pope reaffirms that it is not licit to do evil that good may come of it.

Erroneous theories of morality affect not only the Church but also civil society, as they hinder genuine attempts to improve either. Chapter III of *Veritatis Splendor* comes back to the truth and the light that the truth gives. Universal and unchanging moral norms are at the service of the human person and of human society "because there can be no freedom apart from or in opposition to the truth" (nos. 95–96). True morality is the only possible basis for the renewal of social and political life (no. 98).

Human Dignity in a Personalist Perspective

The fourth contribution of John Paul is a focused emphasis on human dignity. In his moral teaching, there is a pronounced emphasis on human dignity. This is especially so in treating moral questions that involve modern technology: reproductive technologies; medical research and experimentation; questions of genetic engineering and therapy; and some initial statements on ecology.

The argument of "limited dominion" (power, governance, stewardship), for instance, has received much closer attention with the advent of *in vitro* fertilization. The *Catechism* (no. 2377) states that a fundamental objection to *in vitro* fertilization procedures is that they subordinate the origin and destiny of a human person to the dominion or power of technology. There are, of course, other arguments presented: that the unitive and procreative meanings of a marital act are separated, and that procreation is not willed as the fruit of a conjugal act but as the product of a technology. Limits on human dominion over the body and over nature should be set by moral considerations concerning the person, future persons, and the integrity of the human body as the body of a person. Thus, kidnapping, hostage taking, torture, nontherapeutic amputation, mutilation, and direct sterilization are forbidden. Older manuals of theology sometimes applied a principle of limited dominion to at least some of these questions, but the *Catechism* simply states that such actions are contrary to the respect due to the person and contrary to human dignity.

This approach is not entirely new, but it was often explained in different ways. In the past, some would argue that we discover the limits of human dominion over nature by interpreting the natural law. Some saw these limits as set by the natural law and held that they could be determined specifically and in detail by an examination of the biological laws discovered in the human body.

Some made it seem like a relatively simply syllogism: If we examine the human body, we discover certain biological laws. God created the human body with these laws; therefore, God wills that we obey these. If we violate these biological laws, we act against the will of God and thereby sin. This approach was open to criticism from many quarters; some critics called it sheer physicalism.

The Church clearly rejects an interpretation of the natural law in merely biological terms. *Veritatis Splendor* teaches:

> The natural law expresses and lays down the purposes, rights, and duties which are based upon the bodily and spiritual nature of the human person. Therefore, this law *cannot* be thought of as simply a set of norms on the biological level; rather it must be defined as the rational order whereby man is called by the Creator to direct and regulate his life and actions. (no. 50)

The *Catechism* and *Veritatis Splendor* stress again and again one particular aspect of the human person, namely, the body-soul unity as an ontological principle that can serve as a basis for moral norms.

It moves from the ontology of the person as a body-soul unity to establish the relevance of inclination, pointing to where genuine fulfillment is to be found. This locates the traditional theory of the inclinations within an ontology of the person. It then moves to a moral consideration of the person, in particular to respect for the dignity of that person. Respect for the person must include the whole person and not only or simply the moral will of the person. Both the *Catechism* and *Veritatis Splendor* teach that our response to some questions of modern technology must be based on a clear understanding of the integrity and dignity of the human person.

The highly developed Christian personalism and Christian anthropology of John Paul are at the heart of his contributions to moral teaching. His encyclical *Veritatis Splendor* in itself is a seminal contribution to moral theology because it eloquently teaches the truth about the good and the truth about the human person. And moral theology has no other purpose than to teach the truth about the good and the truth about the human person.

John Paul II's Vision of Sexuality and Marriage

The Mystery of "Fair Love"

John F. Crosby

Cardinal John Henry Newman once said, surveying the
history of the Church, that the popes have usually not
taken the initiative in theological inquiry, that it has usually been others who have given the impetus for doctrinal
development, the genius of the Church of Rome showing
itself mainly in a negative way, namely, by critically test-
ing what others propose. Though Newman was able to
produce much historical evidence in support of this general-
ization, he would have surely admitted that the pontificate
of John Paul II represents a great exception. He would have
seen in John Paul II a Pope who has taken the initiative in
theological and philosophical inquiry — who has rethought
traditional teachings with great originality, who has broken
much new ground with his Christian personalism. John Paul
leads the Church, not only as the guardian of the deposit of
the faith, but also as one who has inspired some of the most
fruitful developments in the understanding of the faith. This
rare dimension of papal leadership is nowhere so clearly in
evidence as in John Paul's teaching on man and woman.
Here we have one of the richest legacies of his pontificate.

John F. Crosby is Professor and Chair of Philosophy at Franciscan University of
Steubenville, Ohio.

And yet it is a legacy that is not easy to understand fully. On the one hand, the critics of John Paul denounce him as an obstinate old man who only knows how to say no; they think that in all sexual and marital matters he is only holding the line in a rigid and pastorally insensitive way. They are completely innocent of the originality of his personalist vision of man and woman. On the other hand, the friends and supporters of John Paul, while they do indeed listen respectfully to him and notice the boldness of his teaching on man and woman, are often taken aback and in some cases even slightly scandalized, as when John Paul announced his commitment a few years ago to a "new feminism." The hostile critics need to be challenged to listen to the Pope, and his supporters need to be helped in understanding him. In this essay, I hope to offer something of the needed challenge to the one group as well as something of the needed help to the other.

Karol Wojtyla has had a special affinity for the love between man and woman from the very beginning of his priestly ministry. In his *Crossing the Threshold of Hope* (1994), he writes:

> As a young priest I learned to love human love [by which he means the love between man and woman]. This has been one of the fundamental themes of my priesthood....If one loves human love, there naturally arises the need to commit oneself completely to the service of "fair love," because love is fair, it is beautiful.

And the young Father Wojtyla not only possessed this special affinity for the love between man and woman; early on he also showed an unusual ability to *reflect* on man and woman and the love between them. His first book, *Love and Responsibility,* born of his pastoral experience with young couples, is a deep and original study of "fair love." As archbishop of Krakow, he set up an institute for marriage and family, as he did later in Rome in the first years of his pontificate. He had hardly been elected Pope when he began his famous five-year cycle of Wednesday addresses on man and woman. He was indeed personally called to the celibate life of a priest, which required the sacrifice of renouncing "fair love" in his own life for the sake of the kingdom of God, but he was given a rare gift for understanding this love and even for becoming a kind of prophet of it.

The Personalism of John Paul

The personalism of John Paul is the only possible point of departure for understanding his thought on man and woman. His personalism underlies and informs all his teaching on "fair love," as it underlies and informs all the other regions of his teaching. When John Paul speaks of the "anthropological basis" of his teachings, he is referring to this underlying personalism. Much that seems puzzling in John Paul's teaching on man and woman becomes intelligible as soon as it is traced back to its personalist foundations.

His own way of introducing his personalism is to quote the following sentence from Vatican Council II's Pastoral Constitution on the Church in the Modern World (*Gaudium et Spes*), no. 24: Although man is "the only creature on earth that God has wanted for its own sake," it is nevertheless true that man "can fully discover his true self only in a sincere giving of himself." This passage expresses a fundamental polarity of self-possession and self-donation in the makeup of the human person.

On the one hand, God wills each human being for his own sake, which means that God recognizes each human person as a being of his own, existing in self-possession, as one who cannot exist as a mere part of some whole or as a mere instrumental means for achieving some result. This is why God is the very last one who would use persons in a merely instrumental way, as we can see from the way in which He appeals to and respects our freedom. When we respect each other as persons, giving each other the "space" in which each can be his own end and abstaining from all using in our relations to each other, then we share, the Pope says, in God's vision of human persons.

On the other hand, each human person is made for self-donation, for communion with other persons; this is why he can only find himself by making a sincere gift of himself. We are not *only* beings of our own, belonging to ourselves, as if we were in the end completely closed in upon ourselves, but we are also beings for others, made to exist not only *with* but *for* others, as John Paul puts it. Since God exists as a community of three divine persons, He cannot create an image of Himself in a person who can thrive in solitude; He can only create persons who thrive living in the communion of love with one another.

John Paul adds that there is a genuine polarity here: the self-possession of persons does not interfere with their vocation to interpersonal communion but rather makes it possible. If persons did not belong to themselves, then their union would be subpersonal. Persons are empowered precisely by their self-possession to enter into communion with others. Not only that, but they are never so much themselves as beings of their own as when they share their lives by self-donation.

The Equality of Man and Woman

Aristotle and the Aristotelian tradition in philosophy had denied the equality of man and woman, teaching that the standard case of a human being was the man and that the woman was a "deformed male." Aristotle explained himself in terms of his metaphysics of matter and form, saying that at the conception of a man form dominates matter in the right way, whereas when matter interferes with the due dominance of form the deficient result is the conception of a woman. John Paul disagrees with Aristotle, not only because he knows more about the biology of conception than Aristotle could have known, but above all because he thinks of man and woman in terms of a category unknown to Aristotle, the category of the person. He says that man and woman are both equally persons; the formula of the person used by the Council, which brings together self-possession and self-donation, applies no less to woman than to man. In fact, John Paul has gone so far in this direction as to say that the relation of man and woman in marriage is one of "mutual submission." He has even raised some eyebrows among his supporters by speaking not only of a submission performed by the wife toward her husband, but rather of a mutual submission of husband and wife to each other.

Some critics charge that John Paul has betrayed the equality of man and woman by solemnly teaching that the Church has no authorization to ordain women to the priesthood. He responds that the reservation of the priesthood for men is in no way based on any supposed superiority of man over woman, as in Aristotle. We have here a diversity of roles, which does not imply an inequality of personhood. The fact that God entrusts the conceiving, gestating, and nurturing of a new human being to women rather than to men does not imply that men are inferior as persons. And so if He chooses to entrust a certain sacerdotal function to man rather than to woman, He does not thereby cast woman into a position of inferiority.

This truth about the equality of man and woman has to be balanced by the truth about the complementarity of man and woman. The very principle of their equality, namely, their personhood, is decisively modified by their gender, so that we have masculine and feminine persons. Each gender has its own "genius." As a result, man and woman, for all their equality, are called to complete each other in a unique kind of unity. Nothing could be farther from the mind of John Paul than to affirm equality at the expense of this difference and the complementarity that is based on it. Further on, I will return to this complementarity.

Showing Respect for Man and Woman as Persons

As we saw, the Council taught that each person exists in a sense for his own sake and is therefore willed by God for his own sake. What violates this selfhood of the person is any and every instrumental using of persons. Thus, whenever John Paul asks whether this or that form of man-woman relation involves any using of the one by the other, he is basing himself on this article of his personalism. One may recall the firestorm of ridicule leveled at John Paul in the international press in 1980 when he said in an address that the "adultery in the heart" condemned by Christ can be committed *even within marriage.* From the point of view of his personalism, this is so obvious as to be hardly worth mentioning. The fact that a man and a woman are married to each other is no guarantee at all that in their marital intimacy the one will not use the other as a mere object of gratification. If one of them does use the other like this, then he or she violates the other as person; if their using is mutual then they violate each other. Their being married and even being open to children does not necessarily prevent this violation from occurring. Sexual intimacy is not personalized until in and through it each person affirms and loves the other for his or her own sake.

This much reviled address of John Paul is closely akin to his personalist rethinking of the old idea that one of the purposes of marriage is the *remedium concupiscentiae,* or the relief of concupiscence. This was all too often interpreted to mean that marriage provides the only setting in which selfish sexual concupiscence can be "legally" lived out and burned off and in this way "relieved." It is not too much to say that John Paul abhors any such interpretation. Given his personalism he cannot abide the idea that marriage exists in part to legalize lust. The true "relief of concupiscence," he says, is something altogether different. It is a work of love whereby the sexual energy of a man or woman *is deprived of its selfish sting and made to express and serve spousal love*. Only in this way is sexual love personalized, formed in such a way that man and woman do not sin against the respect due to each other as persons.

The Image of the Triune God in Man and Woman

Let us now consider the other part of the Council's definition of the human person, the part dealing with our vocation to self-donation. John Paul thinks that this vocation is inscribed in our very being by the fact that we are divided into man and woman. There is a complementarity of man and woman that predestines them to a unique kind of love — spousal or conjugal love. In fact, the man-woman difference is for John Paul so intimately connected with the capacity of each human being to love that he is led to make a bold theological move. He sees the image of the triune God in the man-woman difference. Previously, theologians had looked for this image in the soul of each individual human being, commonly following St. Augustine in looking at various triads within each individual soul. It is an entirely new idea to look for the image of God in interpersonal relation, and not just in the most spiritual forms of interpersonal relation, but in the man-woman relation. As far as I know, no Pope before John Paul ever spoke of the image of God in this way: "Man becomes the image of God not so much in the moment of solitude as in the moment of communion," and especially in the communion based on the complementarity of man and woman.

John Paul as the Defender of the Human Body against Its Pagan Detractors

When I cited the Council as teaching that each human person, while being his own, is called to self-donation, I made no mention of the human body. Now in the personalism of John Paul it is all important to understand and to affirm the embodiment of each person. In his view the modern world is not only afflicted by the materialism that reduces man to the body, recognizing nothing else in man but the body; it is also afflicted by a certain aversion to the body — John Paul speaks of a widespread "neo-Manichean culture" — that conceives of persons as estranged from their bodies, as merely using their bodies in an instrumental way. This may be a new idea for many Christians, who perhaps take it for granted that the only real enemy is materialism, but in his great encyclical on moral theology, *Veritatis Splendor,* John Paul traces much of the disorder in present-day moral theology back to the failure to do justice to the embodiment of persons.

Too many of our contemporaries think of the body as raw material available for instrumental use and manipulation by persons. They think that man is at liberty to impose on the body, or abolish from it, whatever meaning he wants. One can see what results when they apply this disparagement of the body to our subject of man and woman. They can think of the gender difference only as an evolutionary product that just happened to come out as it did; compared with the fact that all human beings are persons, the gender difference sinks to the level of the accidental. Man and woman are properly studied in an empirical way by the natural and social sciences, so that all that can be known about man and woman is of a neutral factual nature; there is no metaphysical nature expressed in man and woman, nor any intrinsic value. We persons can make of man and woman whatever we like; we can take the physical "givens" of male and female and can construct masculine and feminine any way we like.

While no Catholic teacher could accept such an account of man and woman, John Paul is distinguished by the depth at which he has overcome it and by the originality with which he has unfolded the truth that our personhood is embodied, and embodied as man and woman, so that all kinds of personal meanings are inscribed in our sexuality.

He has given a personalist rereading of the truth that the
body is not just something physical but something sacramental, that is, a sign, an expression of the person, and
that from the beginning the body in all its masculinity and
femininity participates in the life of the person, indeed, it is
a dimension of the being of each human person.

John Paul's Theology of the Body

In his rich "theology of the body," presented in the first
years of his pontificate (though written before his election),
John Paul unfolds the idea that the vocation of persons to
self-donation, discussed above, is expressed in the bodies
of man and of woman. That it is not good for us to be
alone, that we can find ourselves only through a sincere gift
of ourselves, has its fundamental bodily expression in our
existing as man and woman, and, in fact, cannot really be
understood apart from the difference and complementarity of the sexes. It is as man and woman that we are first
raised out of our solitude, and ordered one to another, and
called to self-donation. The capacity of the masculine body
and of the feminine body to serve self-donation is called by
John Paul the "nuptial meaning" of the human body, a concept that stands at the center of his theology of the body.
Through this nuptial meaning the body is more than biological, more than an object of biological science; it is rather
inserted with all its maleness and femaleness into the life of
the person and so made to be something as truly personal
as it is biological.

It follows that John Paul's approach to the image of God
in man is even more original than we indicated above. For
traditionally one not only looked for this image in each
individual person, but in the soul or spirit of each; John Paul
finds it not only in interpersonal communion, but also in the
bodily masculinity and femininity of men and women. Even
the human body images the triune God, and does so through
its nuptial meaning. Only a God who exists as a communion

of divine persons would create embodied persons who are turned toward each other as man and woman.

John Paul unfolds the self-donation for which man and woman are made by the masculinity and femininity of their bodies. He says that this love, which he calls spousal or conjugal love, is distinguished from all other human love, including even maternal love, by the gesture of self-surrender that belongs to it. In spousal love, self-donation takes the form of self-surrender, that is, of abandoning oneself in love to the other and willing to make oneself belong to the other. Hence the exclusivity of spousal love. There is no room in the human heart for living this self-surrender toward more than one person at the same time. The nuptial meaning of the body stands in the service of this mutual self-surrender. It also stands in the service of nonspousal love, according to John Paul, conditioning as it does all interpersonal communion, but in a unique way it serves spousal love. This is why we can say against the Manichean personalism mentioned above that the body is not something merely biological, merely factual and value-free; it is also made for personal love. Its spousal meaning has not been constructed by us but has been established by God at the creation of man and woman.

With this, we are led to the sexual intimacy of man and woman. For it is in their sexual intimacy that they live and enact in an incomparable way their spousal self-surrender. Indeed, one can hardly understand just what this self-surrender is without referring to the sexual union of man and woman. It is not that spousal self-surrender is nothing but its sexual enactment; it is rather that this self-surrender, in itself something properly personal, finds an irreplaceable expression in the becoming one flesh of man and woman. Whoever abstracts from the bodily being of man and woman and from their bodily union is in no position to understand adequately what spousal self-surrender is, so intimately do the bodily and the spiritual, the biological and the personal, interpenetrate here.

Notice that John Paul speaks here of a meaning of the marital act that is altogether distinct from procreation. For centuries Catholic teachers explained the meaning of it almost exclusively in terms of procreation; only in this century did they begin to explain the marital act in terms of the enactment of spousal love as well. Pius XII was, as far as I can determine, the first Pope who strongly affirmed the love dimension, or as Paul VI called it, the unitive dimension, of the marital act. John Paul has gone well beyond his great predecessors by explaining how this dimension is grounded in the nuptial meaning of the body.

John Paul has not only explored the nuptial meaning of the body, but also, and with great realism, the way in which this meaning gets lost in man-woman relations. The body can, as a result of the fall, so obscure the person that it becomes an impediment to interpersonal communion. With extraordinary depth and originality, John Paul analyzes the way in which a man looks lustfully at a woman, seeing her body without experiencing its nuptial meaning and without seeing the feminine person who should be revealed in it. The body of the woman ceases to be expressive of her as person and so ceases to invite the man to self-donation. In this lustful looking, men see women — and in an analogous way women see men — as objects of selfish consumption rather than as persons to be loved; their look violates the personal selfhood of the other and ignores the fact that each other person is "an enclosed garden," "a fountain sealed" (expressions taken by John Paul from the Song of Songs 4:12 and applied to men and women as persons).

Inspired by Max Scheler's study of shame, John Paul goes on to show that there is a noble sexual shame that is a kind of "personalist instinct" whereby women protect themselves from the lustful concupiscent look of men. His idea is that when a woman realizes that she is an object of male lust, she naturally tries to subdue all that could be sexually provocative about her appearance, not because she fears or despises her sexuality, but because she wants to defuse the male concupiscence that she feels threatening her. The same woman who knows how to feel this sexual shame will have no such reserve about revealing herself to the man who loves her, for she can trust him to look at her so as to see her as person. Of course, the man can also feel shame in this way, but for obvious reasons John Paul gives particular attention to the shame felt by the woman.

In order to retrieve the nuptial meaning of the body for fallen, concupiscent men and women, John Paul in his theology of the body goes back "to the beginning," that is, back to man and woman as they lived their bodily being before the fall. This leads him to his profound analyses of the "original innocence" and the "original nakedness" of man and woman. He says that the first man and woman did not experience any shame in their nakedness because each could see in the body of the other another person and because the attraction of masculinity and femininity stood completely in the service of love. It is not just that they mastered this attraction by strong self-control and made a right use of it by their will; this would express for John Paul an extrinsic dominion of soul over body. Rather, the person dwelt so intimately in the body that the body expressed to the other nothing but the worth and splendor of the person; bodily sexuality was completely absorbed in the energy of spousal love. But with the sin of our first parents a rupture appeared in the body-soul unity; the body now acquired the capacity to obscure the person as well as to reveal him or her; it could now awaken the selfish desire to consume as well as the desire to give oneself spousally; the freedom of original nakedness gave way to the anxiety of feeling shame.

The "redemption of the body," about which John Paul has much to say in his theology of the body, refers to the restoration of the lost integrity of our being. It refers to the reintegration of bodily sexuality and personhood, that is, to the radical "personalization" of masculinity and femininity. The redemption of the body, though it will be consummated in eternity, begins already now in time. Man and woman as they existed in the beginning, and as they will exist in the end, constitute a fundamental norm for men and women now living on earth.

John Paul gives much thought to the eschatological aspects of the theology of the body. In reflecting on the fact that there will be no marriage in the world to come, he asks whether the masculinity and femininity of the body will also be abolished. He answers that it will not; the glorified human bodies will retain their masculinity and femininity and they will retain their nuptial meaning, even if this meaning will not be lived out in the form of marriage. And here we have one of the keys to John Paul's thought on consecrated virginity. He affirms emphatically that the consecrated virgin does not turn away from his or her body with all its nuptial meaning. The renunciation of marriage does not lead to a "neutering" of human beings, for the masculinity and femininity of the body, and its nuptial meaning, are more fundamental than marriage and can serve love in other than marital ways.

Studying the Person through Personal Subjectivity

In explaining the nuptial meaning of the body and other aspects of man and woman, John Paul is constantly speaking of the "subjectivity" of persons. I doubt whether any previous Pope ever spoke of subjectivity. With this, John Paul is referring to the self-experience of persons. But you may ask, why this turn toward self-experience? Why make concessions to the culture of experience, when the task before us is to restore a sense of objective reality, as he has himself stressed in the encyclical *Fides et Ratio* (1998)? We have to answer these questions if we are to understand John Paul on man and woman.

In one of his prepapal studies, Karol Wojtyla distinguishes between what he calls a predominantly "cosmological" understanding of man and a predominantly "personalist" understanding of him. In the former, man is considered from the outside, that is, one stresses the analogies between man and subhuman beings and tries to understand man in terms of categories that are taken from nature and that comprise man along with all kinds of other beings. In the personalist approach, by contrast, one takes man as irreducible to all other beings and explores his identity through those categories that are appropriate precisely to man but not to other beings. Now John Paul teaches that in order to get at that which distinguishes man from everything else — and this is, of course, for him the personhood of man — one must stop looking at man from without and consider how he reveals himself to us from within, that is, how he lives his own being from his own inner center. But this means that we adequately understand man as person only in understanding him in terms of his self-experience, or in other words his interiority.

Considered cosmologically, the meaning of the marital act is primarily procreation; from this point of view, one will be struck by its likeness to subhuman sexual union. Only if we enter into the subjectivity of the marital act do we notice something that has no counterpart in the subhuman animals, namely, the enactment of spousal love. This love dimension of the marital act is not a cosmological fact but a personalist fact; it is found in the self-experience of spouses, in their spousal subjectivity, and it reveals the deep personalist significance of the two in one flesh. Even the procreative meaning of the marital act reveals new and specifically personal dimensions of itself when considered from the point of view of spousal subjectivity.

We find John Paul doing this again and again in his teaching on man and woman: he brings out the personal by consulting the evidence of subjectivity and intersubjectivity. Thus in his magnificent commentary on the Genesis accounts of the creation of man and woman, he notices that one of the two accounts in Genesis 2 is more subjective than the other, that is, it explains man and woman, for instance, in terms of the *solitude* of man before the creation of woman, or in terms of the *shame* they felt before each other after sinning. John Paul centers his commentary primarily on this subjective account; he finds it more congenial to his personalist reading of man and woman. Or recall his analysis of depersonalized sexuality in terms of a certain kind of lustful looking; John Paul is here exploring the subjectivity of fallen sexuality as it expresses itself in this way of looking.

We see, then, that in turning to personal subjectivity John Paul does not fall into subjectivism, but rather finds an all-important resource for developing his profound Christian personalism.

Contraception

John Paul has said that one main incentive for him in developing the theology of the body was the desire to understand more deeply and to give a more convincing account of the Church's so controverted teaching about the wrong of contraception. He teaches that the consummation of spousal love in the sexual intimacy of the spouses, though in itself distinct from procreation, is intrinsically connected with openness to procreation. The fertility of man and woman is not merely biological; it is situated in the realm of their personal love. He proceeds to explain exactly how it is connected with the personal. The bodily expression of spousal love is so intimately united with possible procreation that whenever the marital act is deliberately sterilized *it suffers as an expression of spousal love,* and it begins to be replaced with selfish using. The original insight of John Paul is that openness to new life is not only important for the sake of new life, it is also indispensable for the integrity of the spousal self-donation. Critics of the Church's teaching on contraception typically say that this teaching, when lived, cramps the expression of spousal self-surrender; John Paul responds that this teaching in fact *guarantees* the personalist character of spousal self-surrender.

Some Catholic teachers have been suspicious of the growing recognition of not one but two meanings of the marital act, fearing that the door is opened to contraception if the marital act has some meaning over and above its procreative meaning. They also say that if we must have two meanings of the marital act, then at the very least the procreative meaning must be clearly ranked above the unitive meaning, and they are very worried that John Paul does not even do this, that he simply speaks of them as two equally fundamental meanings. John Paul responds to their concern by saying that the newly recognized unitive meaning is so interrelated with the long recognized procreative meaning that union is compromised if the spouses do not remain open to procreation. Spouses have to remain open to new life not only for the sake of new life but also for the sake of the integrity of their union. This is why his teaching on the unitive meaning of the marital act does not undermine but rather supports the Church's teaching on contraception.

John Paul thinks that people have such a hard time understanding this because, being so used to treating the body as raw material to be instrumentally manipulated for human purposes, they cannot help treating bodily fertility in the same way. If only they can recover a sense of their embodied personhood, and hence of their masculine and feminine personhood, and hence of their paternal and maternal personhood, they will learn to see their fertility in a new personalist light.

The New Feminism of John Paul

Just when his followers thought they had caught up with John Paul and his many original insights into man and woman, he got out ahead of them again just a few years ago when he announced his commitment to a "new feminism." This important new theme of his teaching should not go unmentioned in this essay, especially since many women fear that his teaching on contraception undermines the legitimate concerns of a Christian feminism.

In his feminism, the Pope calls attention to and celebrates what he calls "the genius of woman." He explains this genius in personalist terms, just as we would expect. He says that woman is gifted with a special sense for the concrete person; she is less inclined than man to think of people in terms of stereotypes or of achievements; by nature, she is more sensitive to the *being* rather than the *having* of persons. John Paul makes his own the idea that modern technological civilization is onesidedly masculine and needs nothing so much as the "genius of woman" to protect it from becoming ever more depersonalized. John Paul thinks that it is the maternal vocation of woman, whereby she can receive a new human being into herself, that disposes her to see the person in others. He says that men need to learn from women this sensitivity to persons. He thinks that all the regions of human life, including the life of the Church, will be vastly enriched when the "genius of woman" makes itself much more strongly felt within them. This is why he encourages women to become more present with their femininity in society and in the Church. Of course, he reminds women, in accordance with the whole Catholic tradition, that their contributions to society and the Church should not be made at the expense of their vocation to maternity, and yet he brings something new out of this tradition by saying that the maternal vocation should not be lived at the expense of these contributions. He wants Catholic women to be first of all wives and mothers but then also to be bearers of the "genius of woman" in the contemporary world.

John Paul has gone so far as to apologize to women for the complicity of many Catholics in the neglect and disparagement of the genius of woman over the centuries. In the great ecclesial self-examination that he has initiated as a preparation for the new millennium, he has found something to repent of in the way members of the Church have conducted themselves toward women. He thinks that people in the Church have to be converted from certain patterns of thinking and evaluating if they are going to do justice to the equality of man and woman and to the genius of woman. He speaks of the immeasurable gain that he expects for the Church from a greater presence of woman with her genius.

We see, then, that the Pope's teaching on contraception has nothing to do with confining women to childbearing and child rearing, as if they had no other meaningful tasks besides these.

Conclusion

Now readers can see for themselves why I said at the outset that John Paul has exercised a kind of leadership that the popes have rarely exercised: he has led the people of God in deepening the understanding of man and woman and in bringing to light aspects of man and woman that have not yet received their due. His critics often caricature him as insensitive and inflexible simply because he does not grant them all the sexual license that they want. Too many of them are like ill-mannered children clamoring for some permission from their parents; they have ears only for the yes or no of the parents and are incapable of hearing anything, however thoughtful, that the parents might be saying in explanation of their no. If these critics could only bring themselves to listen to John Paul on man and woman, they would marvel at the freshness and originality of his personalist rereading of sexual and marital morality. They would be astonished at how positive and winning the traditional teachings, reread in John Paul's personalist vein, can become. They had thought that personalism led away from these teachings. Now they have to deal with the challenging fact that in the hands of John Paul personalism leads back to these teachings. The critics of whom I speak, if they were once really to take John Paul seriously, would be forced to admit that he really does understand some of their own deepest concerns and that, as a result of this shared understanding, he convincingly challenges some of their dearest sexual freedoms. They might still not agree with all of his teaching, but they would have to admit that he has done for sexual and marital morality exactly what Vatican Council II wanted to do for the whole Church, namely, to let her enter into closer relation with the "joy and hope, the grief and anguish of the men and women of our time" (*Gaudium et Spes,* no. 1). They may even begin to understand those of us who venerate him as a prophet of the mystery of "fair love."

Chapter 4

Making Sense of the Civilization of Love

John Paul II's Contribution to Catholic Social Thought

RUSSELL HITTINGER

In *Centesimus Annus,* John Paul II writes:

> What we nowadays call the principle of solidarity, the validity of which both in the internal order of each nation and in the international order I have discussed in the encyclical *Sollicitudo Rei Socialis,* is clearly seen to be one of the fundamental principles of the Christian view of social and political organization. This principle is frequently stated by Pope Leo XIII, who uses the term "friendship," a concept already found in Greek philosophy. Pope Pius XI refers to it with the equally meaningful term "social charity." Pope Paul VI, expanding the concept to cover the many modern aspects of the social question, speaks of a "civilization of love."[1]

In order to understand this cluster of notions — solidarity, social charity, the civilization of love — and to

---

RUSSELL HITTINGER is Warren Professor of Catholic Studies and Research Professor of Law at the University of Tulsa.

1. *Centesimus Annus* (1992), no. 3.

appreciate this Pope's contribution to Catholic social teaching, we need to bear in mind two chronic problems that
have occupied, and sometimes preoccupied, the attention of
the popes from the nineteenth century to the present day.
The first problem is the modern state, with its origins in
the revolutions of the eighteenth and nineteenth centuries.
The salient mark of these new regimes was their devotion
to what Leo XIII called "unbounded license" — if not for
individuals (laissez-faire), then for the state, which is the
creature of these individuals (socialism).[2] For the popes,
both the laissez-faire and the socialist states distort the authentic nature of human solidarity. Thus, if the modern
popes appear preoccupied with the modern state, it is not
because they believe that human society is merely a matter
of politics and political order; rather, they see that the new
states have left none of the previous social order untouched.

The second problem was posed by the industrial revolution. The new states revolutionized society from the top, but
the technological and economic developments of the mid-
nineteenth century revolutionized society from below. A
new mass society was being born in the workshops of Eng-
land and the Continent. In the relatively brief span of fifty
years, Rome witnessed the collapse of political Christendom
and then the deep erosion of the solidarity of civil society.

These two problems are the matrix of modern papal social thought. All of the modern popes have wrestled with
them, and each in his own way has made some contribution to understanding the distortions of social order brought
about by modernity. So, before we examine the thought of
John Paul II, let's take a brief look at the history.

The Historical Background

The French Revolution destroyed the political solidarity
of Christendom. It is true, of course, that the Refor-

---

2. *Immortale Dei* (1885), no. 26.

mation had already bruised this "solidarity" by dividing Europe and, eventually, its territories in the New World into opposing religious camps. Even so, the papacy of the Counter-Reformation period relied upon a familiar relationship to the temporal authorities. The familiar model of political solidarity was one of professedly Catholic princes upholding Catholic order domestically and internationally. Whether the individual was a student in Prague or a mestizo in Mexico, the universal principle of citizenship was given in baptism. Men enjoyed a kind of common citizenship rooted in something deeper than the accidents of geography and the often artless transmissions and brutal contests of kingly power.

The new political regimes born in the French Revolution changed everything. The fact that the clergy were forced to commit ecclesiastical treason, that kings were murdered, that popes were kidnapped, bullied, and then forced to cut humiliating deals to protect the few scraps that remained of their temporal estates, traumatized the papacy. Pius VI, who began his pontificate in 1775, warned in his first encyclical that the philosophers of the Enlightenment, "proclaiming that man is born free and subject to no one," were spreading doctrine that would "destroy the bonds of union among men."[3] Pius VI was kidnapped by the French Directory for having condemned civil marriage and divorce, the Civil Constitution of the Clergy (1791), and elevation of the Goddess of Reason as the official religion of the French regime (1793).[4] His successor, Pius VII, quickly issued the encyclical *Diu Satis* (1800) — roughly translated, "Enough already" — comparing Pius VI to Pope St. Martin, who was exiled to the Crimea by the emperor, dying there in 655.

---

3. *Inscrutabile* (1775), no. 7.
4. "We declared that the new Constitution of the Clergy is composed of principles derived from heresy. It is consequently heretical in many of its decrees and at variance with Catholic teaching. In other decrees it is sacrilegious and schismatic. It overturns the rights and primacy of the Church, is opposed to ancient and modern practice, and is devised and published with the sole design of utterly destroying the Catholic religion" (*Charitas* [1791], no. 11).

St. Martin is the last of the popes venerated as a martyr. Of course, Pius VII himself was kidnapped by Napoleon and survived only by diplomatic wit and Napoleon's eventual demise.

The relationship between the Catholic Church and the new regimes began on the sourest possible note; for over a century the popes continued to respond in shock and disgust at those events. In 1864, Pius IX issued, in conjunction with the encyclical *Quanta Cura,* the controversial "Syllabus of Errors," listing some eighty erroneous propositions. More than fifty of the errors listed by Pius IX concerned matters of civil governance. The concluding canon summarizes the spirit of these propositions: it condemned the belief that "the Roman Pontiff can, and ought to, reconcile himself, and come to terms with progress, liberalism, and modern civilization." Pius IX was not reacting in any immediate way to the French Revolution, but to the persistent pattern of political revolutions that engulfed Europe from 1789 onward. Nor was it merely the turmoil but the principles that animated the revolutions that moved the papacy into a reactive stance.

The key point is that the revolutions announced a different universal principle of citizenship — a monistic notion of solidarity that was aggressively secularist. Political citizenship was made the model for everything else. The papacy had no intention of accommodating this new idea of solidarity. When he was still the cardinal archbishop of Imola, Pius VII (1800–1823) had the words "liberty" and "equality" printed on the top of his stationery, but in place of "fraternity" he substituted "And peace in our Lord Jesus Christ."[5] This vignette summarizes what the nineteenth-century popes thought was at stake in the contest with the new regimes. Never was this a mere question of politics but of the ground of human solidarity itself.

---

    5. John Jay Hughes, *Pontiffs: Popes Who Shaped History* (Huntington, Ind.: Our Sunday Visitor, 1994), 165.

The second great event of the modern period was industrialization. It was one thing for the papacy to deal with the new political powers. It was quite another thing, however, to address the problem of the obliteration of the social and cultural forms in which Christian solidarity was embedded. Traditionally, Catholicism knew how to implant itself in the educated, urban classes, as well as in the agrarian classes. Industrialization changed the society underneath the new political institutions. Thus, in the course of only a few decades, the papacy was hit with a double blow. First, the political order changed, and then the social-cultural order changed, also to the great alarm of the papacy.

In the sermons and lectures of Bishop Wilhelm Emmanuel von Ketteler during the 1860s and 1870s, and then in the encyclicals of Leo XIII (1870–1903), the issue of solidarity was reframed as a "social" question. Yet, we cannot forget that the "social" question was never discussed in isolation from the "political" problem. Both Ketteler and Leo XIII insisted that the new states, born in the revolutions, were the cause and the symptom of social atomism. Ketteler declared that "a nation of egotists cannot establish an authority that will represent it in a truly communitarian manner."[6] The distortions evident at the social and economic levels mirrored the flawed foundations of the modern polity, especially the myth of contractarianism (in the English-speaking world) and that of the general will (on the Continent).

"Since there is no such thing as the general popular will," Ketteler argued, "one has to rely on a fiction."[7] Ketteler's critique of the modern state as a "fiction" was adopted by Leo XIII twenty years later. In *Diuturnum*, issued on June 29, 1881, three months after the assassination of Czar Alexander II, who was killed on the very day that he signed a new liberal constitution, Leo vehemently criticized the

---

6. "Liberalism, Socialism, and Christianity," in *The Social Teachings of Wilhelm Emmanuel von Ketteler*, trans. Rupert J. Ederer (Washington, D.C.: University Press of America, 1991), 513.

7. "Labor and the Problem of Christianity," in ibid., 363.

notion that political authority is derived from a contract between men. The following passage is so striking it deserves to be quoted in full.

This power resides solely in God, the Creator and Legislator of all things; and it is necessary that those who exercise it should do it as having received it from God. "There is one lawgiver and judge.... And this is clearly seen in every kind of power... in this way different kinds of authority have between them wonderful resemblances, since, whatever there is of government and authority, its origin is derived from one and the same Creator and Lord of the world, who is God.... Those who believe civil society to have risen from the free consent of men, looking for the origin of its authority from the same source, say that each individual has given up something of his right, and that voluntarily every person has put himself into the power of the one man in whose person the whole of those rights has been centered.... It is plain, moreover, that the pact which they allege is openly a falsehood and a fiction.[8]

What, precisely, was Leo XIII criticizing? Leo was criticizing the great modern myth of the *status naturalis,* according to which individuals create political authority from scratch, as a mere artifact. If political authority is a mere artifact, then so too is the political common good; and if the political common good is a creature of human will, then what is to prevent the rest of the social order from being modeled on that myth? (It is worth remembering that *Rerum Novarum* criticized that very myth insofar as it informed the meaning of contracts in the private sphere: there are some things that one may never freely contract to do).[9]

According to the new regimes, political order comes into being as an instrument for the satisfaction of the interests

8. *Diuturnum* (1881), nos. 11–12.
9. *Rerum Novarum* (1891), nos. 42–45.

of the contractors (or the majority thereof). The state can just as easily absorb everything into itself, making every social institution a tool for the satisfaction of the majority or some abstract notion of the "people," as it can take the opposite route of exercising no public authority for the sake of the weak and vulnerable. In short, the new regimes admit no natural or supernatural common good. Socialism and laissez-faire liberalism are rooted in the same soil.

The ideological and operational atheism of the new regimes was not a new discovery. By the time of the pontificate of Leo XIII, however, that foundational flaw was now seen not only as the ideological cause of the "social" issue but the impediment to solving it. For Leo and his successors, solutions to the social problems brought on by industrialization were being deflected: either by the effort to absorb all power into the state (a false notion of solidarity), or by the effort to hand out private franchises to individuals to make decisions about public or inherently common things (a false notion of subsidiarity).

In *Centesimus Annus,* John Paul strikes more or less the same theme when he criticizes any system that would "suffocate" the human person "between two poles represented by the State and the marketplace."[10] In any event, from the late nineteenth century until the onset of World War II, the papal encyclicals seem rather abruptly to zig and zag: here, pointing out that states exercise too much power; there, criticizing the states for not using sufficient authority to remedy social ills. The regimes made public things private and private things public. Each of these problems was a symptom of a theological error: namely, the effort to create political authority from scratch, without reference to the divine ground of the common good.

In sum, the encyclicals of the modern period found the new regimes wanting. Having witnessed the course of their development for nearly a century, the popes judged that

10. *Centesimus Annus,* no. 49.

they had provided no adequate substitute for Christendom. Bishop Ketteler summarizes this judgment: "When we battle against liberalism, we are fighting for everything that Christianity means to us. We are trying to salvage not only the spiritual heritage of Christendom but even the temporal benefits that have stemmed from it."[11] "Without Christendom," he concluded, "we have only experiments."[12]

Until the papacy of John Paul II, popes continued to appeal to the principles and to the memory of Christendom, where the ruling powers of the temporal sphere vicariously participate in God's rule. Leo XIII asserted that the state is a "likeness and symbol as it were of the Divine Majesty."[13] By dint of participation in God's governance, its ruling powers properly can be called "sacred."[14] When citizens submit to the state, they submit to divine authority, even when the political powers are exercised "by one unworthy."[15] Indeed, in *Rerum Novarum* he expressly calls European peoples back to the "primal constitution" of Christian order.[16] In his mind's eye, Leo still saw the picture of Christendom overseen by Christian princes, who like so many prodigal children need to be summoned back to their princely responsibilities. In *Diuturnum,* he recommends "the institution of the Holy Roman Empire, [which] consecrated the political power in a wonderful manner."[17] Pius XI, in *Quadragesimo Anno* (1931), compared the *civitas* to the mystical body of Christ.[18] In *Quas Primas* (1925), Pius XI established the Feast of Christ the King. Pius XII issued his first encyclical, *Sumi Pontificatus,* on the Feast of Christ the King and declared that the en-

---

11. "Liberalism, Socialism, and Christianity," 514.
12. Ibid., 507.
13. *Sapientiae Christianae* (1890), no. 9.
14. *Immortale Dei* (1885), no. 18.
15. Ibid.
16. *Rerum Novarum*, no. 27. See also *Immortale Dei*, no. 46: "to endeavor to bring all civil society to the pattern and form of Christianity which We have described."
17. *Diuturnum*, no. 23.
18. *Quadragesimo Anno*, no. 90.

tire human race is a "great commonwealth." As well he should, Pius XII explicitly laments the collapse of Christendom, and with it the complex modes of solidarity that were the achievement of the older order.[19] This notion of the state as a "sacred thing" continues through the papacy of Pope John XXIII. In *Pacem in Terris* (1963), Pope John XXIII cites Pius XII: "the dignity of the state's authority is due to its sharing to some extent in the authority of God himself."[20]

It was on this theme of political Christendom that the papal analyses began to flag. The papal diagnosis of the problems that attend the modern state were well focused and generally were philosophically astute. But what is the alternative? Leo XIII and Pius X could refer to Christian princes, or at least to some semblance of Christian political order, for at the time of World War I there were still seventeen European monarchies. By the end of the war, however, the older order was completely destroyed. It is significant that Pius XI and Pius XII, while proclaiming Christ the King, do not speak of the kingly or sacred powers of the prince. *Quas Primas* speaks rather of the duties of "nations," "kingdoms," and "parliaments" to recognize the kingship of Christ.[21]

What must the social order look like in the absence of Christian princes? In his very important and influential essay "Freedom, Authority and the Church" (1862), Ketteler

---

19. Consider, for example: "The denial of the fundamentals of morality had its origin, in Europe, in the abandonment of that Christian teaching of which the Chair of Peter is the depository and exponent. That teaching had once given spiritual cohesion to a Europe which, educated, ennobled, and civilized by the Cross, had reached such a degree of civil progress as to become the teacher of other peoples, of other continents ... and the much vaunted civilization of society, which has made ever more rapid progress, withdrawing man, the family, and the State from the beneficent and regenerating effects of the idea of God and the teaching of the Church, has caused to reappear, in regions in which for many centuries shone the splendors of Christian civilization, in a manner ever clearer, ever more distinct, ever more distressing, the signs of a corrupt and corrupting paganism" (*Sapientiae Christianae*, nos. 29–30).

20. *Pacem in Terris*, no. 47.

21. *Quas Primas*, nos. 25–26.

praised Christian kingship as the model that best protects
natural and supernatural solidarity in the body politic.[22] At
the same time, he had to admit that the modern practice
of monarchy (by Catholics and Protestants) had "become
nothing more than a destructive idolatry."[23] He understood
perfectly well that modern monarchies were prepared to
invoke God for no other purpose than blessing what was
essentially a human artifact. In this respect, monarchical
order did not necessarily differ from the radical myth that
social order is constructed by human will.[24] Ketteler and
the popes rejected mechanical constitutionalism in favor
of corporatism.[25] They held that all levels of society, from
government to families, are joined together by instrinsically
valuable modes of solidarity and common goods rather than
by self-interest checked and pacified by the external fences
of written constitutions. But Ketteler, the greatest of all
the corporatists, admitted: "Today, of course, the corpo-
rate structure would have to take on entirely different form
than during the Middle Ages."[26]

The search for a corporatist model seemed thwarted at
every turn. By the 1930s, the economic and political life
of western nations had become more and more centralized.
When *Quadragesimo Anno* was issued in 1931, the Great
Depression had begun, and enlightened opinion everywhere
clamored for stronger exercises of government authority.
The corporatist ideal also ran into the problem of fascism,
an ideology that also appealed to the ideal of organic society
rather than to the more external and mechanical rule of law
characteristic of constitutional democracies.

---

22. "Freedom, Authority and the Church," in *The Social Teachings of Wilhelm
Emmanuel von Ketteler*, trans. Rupert J. Ederer (Washington, D.C.: University
Press of America, 1991), 149–58.
23. Ibid., 145.
24. Ibid., 146.
25. Ibid., 195–97.
26. Ibid., 197.

Pius XII to John Paul II

World War II made the papacy take a second look at the ideal of constitutional democracy. In his Christmas message of 1942, Pius XII notes that the particular institutional forms of domestic and international politics are not the business of the Church — so long as "these forms conform to the law of God." The "law of God" is put in this way:

> From individual and social life we should rise to God, the First Cause and Ultimate Foundation, as He is the Creator of the first conjugal society, from which we have the society which is the family, and the society of peoples and of nations. As an image, albeit imperfect, of its Exemplar, the One and Triune God, Who through the Mystery of the Incarnation, redeemed and raised human nature, life in society, in its ideals and in its end, possesses by the light of reason and of revelation a moral authority and an absoluteness which transcend every temporal change.[27]

Interestingly, the sovereign state does not even make a cameo appearance in this scheme of the great-chain-of-being. In his Christmas message of 1944, Pius XII recommends (albeit tinctured with caution) the external fences of constitutionalism — one power checking another — but only so long as government respects the dignity of the human person and the dignity of his labor, and so long as social unity be regarded as intrinsic and as expressing natural norms that cannot be reduced to the mechanism of the institutions of the state. He concedes that, after the experience with dictatorships, democracy "appears to be a

---

27. Delivered six months before promulgation of the encyclical *Mystici Corporis* (June 29, 1943). This encyclical develops what may be called a solidarist, rather than a merely juridical, understanding of atonement. We see the move toward thicker, more solidarist conceptions of society and Church, and the beginning of a thinner, more juridical conception of the state.

postulate of nature imposed by reason itself."[28] He says that the world would not have been "dragged into the vortex of a disastrous war" had there been "efficient guarantees in the people themselves."[29]

Thus, Pius made an important revision in the papal analysis of the modern state. Pius saw that, despite the flawed ideological pedigree of the modern states, the despotic and totalitarian states made it necessary to appeal to certain principles internal to modern constitutional democracies. Jacques Maritain, writing just a few years after Pius XII's 1944 Christmas allocution, contrasts "instrumentalist" with "substantialist" conceptions of the state. The substantialist theory pictures the state as a moral person, a subject of right, and consequently a "whole."[30] Throughout the late nineteenth and early twentieth centuries, there was a danger that the older papal view of sacral kingship would be confused with substantialism. For sacral kingship does, in a way, represent the "whole" of the people. King James I told Parliament in 1603: "I am the husband, and all the whole island is my lawful wife; I am the head, and it is my body; I am the shepherd and it is my flock." The older model represented political authority as a communion. Kings were given a ring as a sign of their marriage to the kingdom. This kind of husbandly responsibility, however, is certainly not what Mussolini had in mind when he declared that "everything is in the State, and nothing human or spiritual exists, much less has value outside the State." Mussolini did not have a marriage in mind, but a rape, a totalization and reduction of human social reality to the state.[31]

---

28. "1944 Christmas Message of His Holiness Pope Pius XII: Addressed to the People of the Entire World on the Subject of Democracy and a Lasting Peace," no. 19.

29. Ibid., no. 12.

30. Jacques Maritain, *Man and the State* (Chicago: University of Chicago Press, 1951), 13–14. Maritain, however, does not give up the older papal criticism that the modern state rests upon a "fiction." See note 11 on p. 16. Pius XII, too, continues the Leonine critique of the modern state as "fiction." In his 1942 Christmas address, he refers to "superimposed and fictitious" order.

31. David Nicholls, *Deity and Domination: Images of God and the State in*

Whatever the virtues of the older model, by the mid-twentieth century it could not be reasserted without confusing it with a totally different creature: the secular notion of state absolutism and sovereignty. Maritain argued that the state is but one part of the body politic, namely, that part concerned with the maintenance of law, the promotion of the common welfare, and the administration of public things. The state is an instrument of, rather than the substance of, human solidarity.

The gravitation of papal social theory away from solidarist conceptions of the state is evident in *Gaudium et Spes.* Consider the following passages:

> As for public authority, it is not its function to determine the character of the civilization, but rather to establish the conditions and to use the means which are capable of fostering the life of culture among all even within the minorities of a nation. It is necessary to do everything possible to prevent culture from being turned away from its proper end and made to serve as an instrument of political or economic power.... The political community exists, consequently, for the sake of the common good, in which it finds its full justification and significance, and the source of its inherent legitimacy. Indeed, the common good embraces the sum of those conditions of the social life whereby men, families, and associations more adequately and readily may attain their own perfection.[32]

The minimizing of the solidarist state and the maximizing solidarist social order reaches it apogee in *Centesimus Annus* (1991). It teaches that human participation in sacral powers is reserved for the individual and the family, invariably in contrast to the powers of the state:

---

the *Nineteenth and Twentieth Centuries* (London and New York: Routledge, 1989), 90.

32. *Gaudium et Spes,* nos. 59, 74.

> The root of modern totalitarianism is to be found in
> the denial of the transcendent dignity of the human
> person who, as the visible image of the invisible God, is
> therefore by his very nature the subject of rights which
> no one may violate — no individual, group, class, na-
> tion, or state. Not even the majority of a social body
> may violate these rights by going against the minor-
> ity, by isolating, oppressing, or exploiting it, or by
> attempting to annihilate it.[33]

Note that there is no theological mantle draped over the
state. The first and most persistent limit upon the state is
the "transcendent dignity" of the human person who is the
image of God.

In *Centesimus Annus,* John Paul treats the modern state
as potentially dangerous concentration of coercive power
that uproots the "subjectivity of society" and makes itself coincident with the common good. Significantly, the
Pope maintains that the decentralization of power and responsibility must be sought "even though it may weaken
consolidated power structures."[34] Interestingly, it is precisely in the paragraph where the Pope emphasizes that
the power of the state will be weakened that he introduces
the notion of the "progressively expanding chain of solidarity."[35] The state is not the end of human society. The
state's main job is to establish a rule of law as a sort of um-
brella under which the natural and voluntary societies can
achieve their purposes and distinctive forms of communion.
Solidarity is not the same thing as the juridical state.

John Paul frequently refers to the idea of a "civilization
of love" — a phrase used by Paul VI in his social encyclicals.
But when John Paul II uses the term, he is careful to distinguish between society and culture on the one hand and the

---

33. *Centesimus Annus*, no. 44. See also no. 22.
34. Ibid., no. 43.
35. Ibid.

state on the other. Take, for example, his *Letter to Families* (February 2, 1994):

> Dear families, the question of responsible fatherhood and motherhood is an integral part of the "civilization of love," which I now wish to discuss with you. . . . The phrase is linked to the tradition of the "domestic church" in early Christianity, but it has a particular significance for the present time. Etymologically the word "civilization" is derived from "civis" ("citizen"), and it emphasizes the civic or political dimension of the life of every individual. But the most profound meaning of the term "civilization" is not merely political, but rather pertains to human culture. Civilization belongs to human history because it answers man's spiritual and moral needs. Created in the image and likeness of God, man has received the world from the hands of the Creator, together with the task of shaping it in his own image and likeness. The fulfillment of this task gives rise to civilization, which in the final analysis is nothing else than the "humanization of the world."[36]

As these sentences suggest, the notion of a "civilization of love" is applied chiefly to the ecclesiological and familial orders and, through them, to culture. The Pope nowhere suggests that the juridical state is or ought to be portrayed in such terms; in fact, in the *Letter to Families,* he questions the idea of the state as a "greater" society.

In one of his earliest encyclicals, *Familiaris Consortio* (1981), signed on the Feast of Christ the King, John Paul explains that the rights of the family are grounded in a sacramental kingship whereby married people participate in the triplex *munus Christi* (duty or mission of Christ), an office that devolves in varying modalities upon the people of God and, most fully, of course, on the Pope and bishops. Kingship, however, devolves on the royal priestly laity to

---

36. *Letter to Families*, no. 13.

such an extent that it can be said with respect to them that "the social and political role is included in the kingly mission of service in which Christian couples share by virtue of the sacrament of marriage, and they receive both a command which they cannot ignore and a grace which sustains and stimulates them."[37]

Solidarity and the Civilization of Love

What is a *civis?* The papal answer remains remarkably consistent. A *civis* is a human person whose dignity is grounded in *imago Dei* and whose identity is to be found in modes of solidarity that the political state exemplifies only in an incomplete manner.

Yet, solidarity is an inherently complex notion. Solidarity can mean: (1) common material things, which are subject to distributive justice; (2) sociological or economic states of affairs, such as technological and economic interdependence; (3) personal attitudes, dispositions, or virtues with regard to what is, or should be, common; (4) activities, in the sense of teamwork and collaboration toward common ends; (5) loving communion between persons, where the communion is the very goal of action. "Common" is amenable to quite diverse and indeed, equivocal, meanings. Think, for example, of the disparate ways we call a thing, a place, an activity, or a nature "common."

For John Paul, the common good can consist of goods realized in individuals, which are called "common" by virtue of a common species. For example, human beings share a common humanity, even though there is no "humanity" existing independently of individuals, nor a "humanity" distributed to persons. This ontological perfection is only "in" individuals; so, from individuals we gather the predicate that is common. By virtue of our common

---

37. *Familiaris Consortio*, no. 47. See George Huntston Williams, *The Contours of Church and State in the Thought of John Paul II* (Waco, Tex.: Institute of Church-State Studies, Baylor University Monograph Series, 1983), 70–71.

humanity, three notions arise: (1) common status, in the sense that no person is more or less human than another; (2) common perfections, such as health, knowledge, and religious devotion; (3) common utilities, such as money, food, and technology. Each of these can be the ground of moral and legal rights; each can express a reason for solidarity. In *Sollicitudo Rei Socialis* (1987), the "virtue" of solidarity is described (initially) as the willingness to make a moral response to common goods as we have just described them:

> It is above all a question of interdependence, sensed as a system determining relationships in the contemporary world in its economic, cultural, political and religious elements, and accepted as a moral category. When interdependence becomes recognized in this way, the correlative response as a moral and social attitude, as a "virtue," is solidarity.[38]

Thus, when John Paul II speaks of "solidarity toward society's weakest members,"[39] he emphasizes our common humanity, which prohibits us from cutting corners in the distribution of legal rights and economic resources, or, in other words, common activities.

Perhaps the most evident example of common goods as common activities is the political order itself, that is, the body politic. Above I noted the emergence in Roman documents of the instrumentalist conception of the state. The state is not the substance of the common good, but its servant. This means that the state cannot (or should not) act unilaterally. By definition, a despotic regime is one in which the parts — the governed — have no power of resistance. Political order is inherently collaborative; take away the common activity, and at least one kind of important common good is removed. Other goods might remain, but not the political good.

---

38. *Sollicitudo Rei Socialis,* no. 38.
39. *Evangelium Vitae,* no. 8.

The notions of "collaboration," "cooperation," the "spirit of creative initiative," and the "expanding chain of solidarity" express, in different ways, and at different levels, common goods as common activities. Depending on the particular encyclical, the idea of solidarity as common activities is applied to domestic political order, international relations, the initiatives of intermediate societies, and economic life. In *Centesimus Annus*, John Paul writes:

> By means of his work a person commits himself, not only for his own sake but also for others and with others. Each person collaborates in the work of others and for their good. One works in order to provide for the needs of one's family, one's community, one's nation, and ultimately all humanity. Moreover, a person collaborates in the work of his fellow employees, as well as in the work of suppliers and in the customers' use of goods, in a progressively expanding chain of solidarity.[40]

Here, the theme of subsidiarity comes into view. It is true, of course, that subsidiarity can arise within the first set of meanings: for example, only the individual can exercise his or her own conscience, and, all things being equal, the community must respect that action at its proper level. The president can establish a commission on the health of American youth, but at the end of the day, health is achieved only if the individual exercises his body. So, the idea of subsidiarity is seminally present in that first complex of meanings, running from common nature, to common perfections, to common utilities. But, once we emphasize the common good as a common activity, the idea of subsidiarity really becomes a useful concept in social theory.

If the common good is constituted by the common activity, then whenever "higher" powers intervene in such a

---

40. *Centesimus Annus*, no. 43.

way that the common activity is supplanted, or whenever the result of common activity is achieved behind the back, as it were, of the collaborative activity itself, the good is lost. Take, for example, the common activities that go into the work of an orchestra. Every part needs to be harmonized with the others in order to produce the desired result. If the good being aimed at were simply the external result, however, then there is no reason, other than aesthetic preference, why a computer-generated concerto would not suffice. It is at least plausible that the common activity constitutes part of the good being aimed at. The attunement of one free agent to another is a distinctive kind of common good.

Therefore, it seems that a truly useful concept of subsidiarity depends upon a concept of solidarity (or, of the common good) that preserves the intrinsic value of collaborative activity. Without that value, discussion about subsidiarity easily becomes, as in our American policy debates over "federalism," an issue of magnitudes concerning money and power. Suppose, for example, that a policy expert could show that "welfare" is most efficiently accomplished by subcontracting the work to a private firm. Would we be missing anything by commissioning others to do this work? The same question can be asked with respect to a wide array of collaborative activities, from education to the deliberative councils of a legislature. If solidarity were restricted to the first set of notions (common nature, perfections, and utilities) we could satisfy (hypothetically) the requirements of the common good by adopting whatever policies most efficiently distribute the useful goods.

Here it is appropriate to introduce John Paul's understanding of the "subjectivity" of society. In *Centesimus Annus*, he refers to the subjectivity of society in terms of "structures of participation and shared responsibility."[41] He writes:

---

41. *Centesimus Annus*, no. 46.

> The social nature of man is not completely fulfilled in the State, but is realized in various intermediary groups, beginning with the family and including economic, social, political and cultural groups which stem from human nature itself and have their own autonomy, always with a view to the common good. This is what I have called the "subjectivity" of society which, together with the subjectivity of the individual, was canceled out by "Real Socialism."[42]

Notice that the argument against socialism is not chiefly an argument about its inefficiency, namely, that the common good, as a just distribution of resources, was not met. Rather, what was "canceled out" was the common good(s) constituted by free, collaborative agents.

The expressions "subjectivity of society" and "expanding chain of solidarity" often sit adjacent to yet another idea of common good. John Paul's definition of the virtue of solidarity as a certain moral attitude taken toward interdependence is developed further in *Sollicitudo Rei Socialis:*

> Solidarity is undoubtedly a Christian virtue. In what has been said so far it has been possible to identify many points of contact between solidarity and charity, which is the distinguishing mark of Christ's disciples. ... Beyond human and natural bonds, already so close and strong, there is discerned in the light of faith a new model of the unity of the human race, which must ultimately inspire our solidarity. This supreme model of unity, which is a reflection of the intimate life of God, one God in three Persons, is what we Christians mean by the word "communion."[43]

A distinct notion has been added to the idea of a common good. Although this third range of meanings is almost

---

42. Ibid., no. 13. See also *Sollicitudo Rei Socialis,* no. 15.
43. *Sollicitudo Rei Socialis,* no. 40.

always discussed in theological terms, the idea of a common good *as* communion, where the communion is the very good being aimed at, is at least somewhat intelligible on its own terms. To be sure, marriage is at least a matter of collaborative activities. But a marriage can be understood as something more than a common good constituted by collaborative activity. It is also a communion, a one flesh unity. Married people can use their relationship as a useful means for the distribution of goods (for themselves, for children, and for wider society); married people also constitute an essential cell, indeed a model, for the goods of mutual deliberation; but if they do not achieve the unity of one flesh they simply do not do what married people do *qua* married. For the Catholic Church, marriage is a sign and instrument of the union of God and man.[44]

The encyclicals and conciliar documents speak of "spiritual unity," or "interior unity," or "communion" typically in reference to marriage, eucharistic fellowship, and baptism, through which the individual is grafted into the body of Christ. The "civilization of love" includes all of the diverse notions of common good, not just the theological one. But the theological concept of communion is the main model for what the papacy means by the proposition that man is inherently social. The papal Magisterium has never proposed that the common good can be properly considered or achieved without supernatural charity. In short, this understanding of the common good as communion is not simply introduced to complete the picture, as though communion were an addendum to political and economic realities. All of the meanings of "common" are ordered to common good as communion; and when we read the present Pope's discussion of the family, it would seem that the diverse notions of "common" proceed from communion.[45]

---

44. Cf. ibid., no. 31.

45. "As a person, one can give oneself to another person or to other persons, and ultimately to God, who is the author of our being and who alone can fully

Solidarity as the Basis of the Political Order

The relocation of the sacral principle (participation in divine, kingly authority) away from the state is the great interpretative matrix for contemporary papal social theory. John Paul, a Pole who suffered first-hand from totalitarian regimes of both the political Left and Right, has brought that line of thought to fruition. From Pius XII and the documents of Vatican Council II, he inherits and then develops the analytical tools and language for making sense of a postpolitical Christendom: a solidarist conception of the social order, even of the body politic, protected by a distinctively modern conception of a juridical or instrumentalist state. All the while, John Paul continues the papal critique of the modern "fiction," namely, that social order is a creature of contracts, as though common rights, activities, and social communion were mere artifacts. In his later encyclicals, *Veritatis Splendor* (1993) and *Evangelium Vitae* (1995), he criticizes that very myth in ways reminiscent of the nineteenth-century popes.

The popes of the nineteenth century were convinced that authentic solidarity is incompatible with the instrumentalist state, but they could point to no concrete alternative. John Paul takes the modern state in its best light and shows how it is compatible with a solidarist social order and the civilization of love. Yet, this relocation of the sacral principle from kings to society presents a host of new difficulties, not the least of which is the problem of persuading secular regimes to recognize sacral principles from below as it were. The recent historical record would seem to indicate that temporal authorities are no more prepared today to recog-

---

accept our gift. A person is alienated if he refuses to transcend himself and to live the experience of self-giving and of the formation of an authentic human community oriented toward his final destiny, which is God. A society is alienated if its forms of social organization, production, and consumption make it more difficult to offer this gift of self and to establish this solidarity between people" (*Centesimus Annus*, no. 41).

nize the sacral principle from below, than their ancestors were prepared to recognize it from above.

In the twilight of his pontificate, specifically, in the encyclical *Evangelium Vitae*, John Paul warns that authentic solidarity is not compatible with the way the democracies understand themselves today. For these states have made life and death subject to the myth of the social contract; indeed, the states are acting more or less as the nineteenth-century popes said they would act. They recognize no ruling power higher or lower than themselves. In *Evangelium Vitae* (1995), he speaks ominously of a "conspiracy"[46] against human rights; he refers to the "disintegration" of these governments[47] and characterizes them as "tyrant states";[48] he accuses them of poisoning the "culture of rights";[49] of having reversed the "long historical process leading to the discovery of the idea of human rights"; of violating the "principles of their own constitutions"; and, what seems new when measured against even the vicissitudes of the nineteenth century, he asserts that there is an obligation to disobey constitutionally legitimate authorities. One is especially struck by the Pope's use in *Evangelium Vitae* of Exodus 1:17. Recounting the story of the Egyptian midwives who defied Pharaoh because, as the scripture notes, "they feared God," the Pope urges resistance to the temporal powers' usurpation of God's authority over life and death.[50]

Time will tell whether John Paul II has charted out the principles of a new social order, a civilization of love that comports with a modern understanding of limited government, or whether he has completed a line of papal thought that has brought the Church, once again, into conflict with the secular regimes.

---

46. *Evangelium Vitae*, no. 12.
47. Ibid., no. 20.
48. Ibid.
49. Ibid., no. 18.
50. Ibid., no. 73.

❧ Chapter 5 ❧

Reorienting the Church on the Eve of the Millennium
John Paul II's New Evangelization
DAVID L. SCHINDLER

History will recognize the pontificate of Pope John Paul II as the watershed moment in the interpretation of Vatican Council II. And history will recognize the heart of this interpretation to be a new sense of the *imago Dei* resulting from the integration of trinitarian Christology and anthropology.

The "newness" of John Paul's achievement can be best understood when his christocentrism is read as a hermeneutic of *Gaudium et Spes (GS)*, and hence as a conscious clarification of issues discussed already at the Council.

ABBREVIATIONS

CCC	*Catechism of the Catholic Church*
CTH	*Crossing the Threshold of Hope*
DH	*Dignitatis Humanae*
EV	*Evangelium Vitae*
GS	*Gaudium et Spes*
ICFL	*Instruction on Christian Freedom and Liberation*
LTK	*Lexikon für Theologie und Kirche*
PESC	Weber, *The Protestant Ethic and the Spirit of Capitalism*
RH	*Redemptor Hominis*
RM	*Redemptoris Missio*
SRS	*Sollicitudo Rei Socialis*

DAVID L. SCHINDLER is Editor-in-Chief of *Communio* and Gagnon Professor of Fundamental Theology at the John Paul II Institute for Studies on Marriage and Family, Washington, D.C.

Gaudium et Spes concludes its introduction with the following powerful statement:

> In the face of modern developments there is a growing body of men who are asking the most fundamental of all questions or are glimpsing them with a keener insight: What is man? What is the meaning of suffering, evil, death, which have not been eliminated by all this progress? What is the purpose of these achievements, purchased at so high a price? What happens after this earthly life is ended?
>
> The Church believes that Christ, who died and was raised for the sake of all [cf. 2 Cor. 5:15], can show man the way and strengthen him through the Spirit in order to be worthy of his destiny: nor is there any other name under heaven given among men by which they can be saved [cf. Acts 4:12]. The Church likewise believes that the key, the center, and the purpose of the whole of man's history is to be found in its Lord and Master. . . . And that is why the Council, relying on the inspiration of Christ, the image of the invisible God, the firstborn of all creation [cf. Col. 1:15], proposes to speak to all men in order to unfold the mystery that is man and cooperate in tackling the main problems facing the world today. (no. 10)

The Church's basic purpose in *Gaudium et Spes* is to initiate a dialogue with the modern world, in order to offer service to the whole human family (cf. nos. 1–3). The Church carries out this purpose by addressing the problems facing humankind "in the light of the Gospel" and "with the saving resources which the Church has received from its founder under the promptings of the Holy Spirit." Thus,

> it is man himself who must be saved: it is mankind that must be renewed. It is man, therefore, who is the key to this discussion, man considered whole and entire, with body and soul, heart and conscience, mind and will.

> This is the reason why this sacred Synod, in pro-
> claiming the noble destiny of man and affirming an
> element of the divine in him, offers to cooperate unre-
> servedly with mankind in fostering a sense of brother-
> hood to correspond to this destiny of theirs. (no. 3)

For John Paul, the relation between anthropology and
Christology is key to understanding the missionary task of
the Church.

During the Council, several issues were raised concerning the relationship between anthropology and Christology.
The most important of these are highlighted by Cardinal Joseph Ratzinger in his 1968 commentary on the
anthropology of *Gaudium et Spes.* [1] He raises questions regarding certain of the Pastoral Constitution's formulations,
but his critical comments nonetheless all point toward an
emphatically positive conclusion regarding the anthropological achievement of the document. His questions identify
ambiguities in the text, for the purpose of integrating
and thereby strengthening the text in light of the striking
christological-anthropological summary offered in this final
paragraph.

It is important to note in this connection that the need to
clarify further the meaning of conciliar statements is the rule
and not the exception in the history of the Church. It should
therefore come as no surprise — and cause no scandal —
that further clarification is indicated in the case of Vatican
Council II. As Walter Kasper has made clear, it is characteristic of councils often to leave statements juxtaposed that
seem to stand in tension with one another, for further development by the Church and her theologians.[2] With respect to

1. See his "Kommentar zum I. Kapitel," in *Lexikon für Theologie und Kirche*
(*LTK*), ed. H. Vorgrimler (Freiburg: Herder, 1968), 14:313–54. For an English
translation, see *Commentary on the Documents of Vatican II,* ed. H. Vorgrimler
(New York: Herder and Herder, 1969), 5:115–63. References to page numbers
will be given for both the English and German texts.
2. Kasper, *Theology and the Church* (New York: Crossroad, 1989), 166–76.
Kasper says that it is "completely in the conciliar tradition for a juxtaposition to

Vatican II, Kasper gives as an example its "juxtaposition," "double viewpoint," or "dialectic" between "a traditional hierarchical ecclesiology and a new...*communio* ecclesiology."[3] One might add to the list of conciliar examples Chalcedon, with its christological affirmation of two natures coincident with one person, or the Council of Trent on grace and freedom and justification, or Nicea, with its *homoousion.*

None of these councils ended — or could end — the need for further theological clarification, even if they all provided formulas essential for establishing ecclesial parameters for that clarification. The pertinent point here is that critical reflection that implies dissent from conciliar teaching must be distinguished from critical reflection that seeks rather to resolve what are real questions prompted by the text itself — for the purpose then of embracing the authentic meaning of the text.

Gaudium et Spes is the longest document in the entire history of Church councils. It is also the first document of the Magisterium to speak so directly about the temporal aspects of Christian life, and about human beings coming to terms with the problems of their earthly lives. At the heart of the document's effort to discern the signs of the times is an anthropology inspired by the vision of humanity in Jesus Christ, a vision of the *imago Dei.* In his commentary, Ratzinger highlights several issues pertinent to this Christ-centered understanding of the *imago Dei.* Ratzinger points out that the creational context within which the image of God is situated lacks any mention of Jesus

---

remain. As in the case of every council, the theoretical mediation of these positions is a task for the theology that comes afterward" (171). My "Christology and the *Imago Dei:* Interpreting *Gaudium et Spes," Communio* 23 (Spring 1996): 156–84, discusses, in light of the principle recorded by Kasper, the tension between the "theistic" emphasis of *GS,* no. 12, and the "christocentric" emphasis of *GS,* no. 22 (a tension which Kasper himself refers to as *eine gewisse Unschärfe* ["a certain lack of clarity"]: cf. his "The Theological Anthropology of *Gaudium et Spes," Communio* 23 (Spring 1996): 129–40.

3. Kasper, *Theology and the Church,* 170.

Christ. It lacks a New Testament context. Instead of choosing an explicitly christological and historical starting point, the Pastoral Constitution begins with what Ratzinger terms a "theistically-colored and to a large extent non-historical view" (120; *LTK,* 317).

Ratzinger notes that, although revisions had been made in the Ariccia draft (Text 4 of what was to become *Gaudium et Spes*), in response to objections on this matter, the final document retains its original starting point. While acknowledging the legitimacy of a less historical starting point (one that advances "from outside inward," he says that this original framework is linked with ambiguities that remain in the final text.[4]

Paragraph 12 of *Gaudium et Spes* signals man's dominion over all earthly creatures as foundational for human dignity. For Ratzinger, it is crucial to see that this dominion as understood in the document is the consequence and not the content of the image of God (121–22; *LTK,* 318). The content, he says, as indicated by St. Augustine, is the capacity for God. Augustine emphasizes the dynamic aspect of the idea of human person as the image of God: the person is the image of God to the extent that he or she moves toward God, and he disfigures this image to the extent that he turns away from God. In a word, dominion properly

---

4. For an overview of the discussion at the Council on the issue raised here by Ratzinger and the role especially of the German bishops in this discussion, see Charles Moeller, "History of the Constitution," *Commentary on the Documents of Vatican II,* ed. Vorgrimler, 5:1–77, at 59–61. Moeller summarizes the two main tendencies which "had stood confronted since the beginning of work on Schema 13 [*Gaudium et Spes*]: one a concrete outlook marked by a certain fundamental optimism, the other a dialectical, paradoxical attitude insisting on the polyvalency of the world in which the Church lives" (no. 60). Moeller highlights the importance of this discussion (and in particular of the meeting that took place on September 17, 1965, regarding the Ariccia text, at which Ratzinger was present as a theological expert): "In fact [the meeting] was decisive because it meant that all revisions during the last two stages were made on the general lines that a balance must be struck between the opposing tendencies of the two ways of envisaging the problem.... As a consequence, the final text doubtless lost a little of its homogeneity, its continuous movement forward, in favour of a presentation which multiplied contrasts. But it gained in wealth of content and complexity. In short, it acquired a more dialectical character" (no. 61).

understood consists in ordering things in light of the person's capacity for worship, hence in integrating them into the glorification of God. The person is a liturgist before he or she is a worker.[5]

Ratzinger notes that the "clearly stated difference between content and consequence of man's creation to the image of God implies an affirmation which has not been sufficiently taken into account in postconciliar discussion" (122; *LTK*, 318).

Ratzinger argues that the omission of Christology from the Pastoral Constitution's original approach to anthropology imposes its consequences in the Constitution's treatment of freedom in paragraph 17. This whole text, he says, gives scarcely a hint of the discord that runs through the human person and which is described so dramatically by St. Paul. Indeed, the text falls into "downright Pelagian terminology" when it says that man "*sese ab omni passionum captivitate liberans, finem suum* in boni libera electione *persequitur et apta subsidia* efficaciter ac sollerti industria sibi *procurat*" (138; *LTK*, 332).[6] Ratzinger insists that the phrase added in the next sentence, *plene actuosam* — namely, that, having been weakened by sin, the person needs the help of God's grace to make his relationship to his end "fully actual" — does not suffice to rectify the problem. Indeed, this phrase, he says, confirms that at best a "semi-Pelagian representational pattern has been retained" (138; *LTK*, 332).

---

5. Regarding the nature of dominion as "consequence," cf. the Sacred Congregation for the Doctrine of the Faith's *Instruction on Christian Freedom and Liberation* (*ICFL*, 1986): "In this vocation to exercise dominion over the earth by putting it at his service through work, one can see an aspect of the image of God (Gen. 1:27–28). But human intervention is not 'creative'; it encounters a material nature which like itself has its origin in God the Creator and of which man has been constituted the 'noble and wise guardian' (cf. *Redemptor Hominis* [*RH*], no. 15)" (no. 34).

6. The italicized words are those explicitly referred to by Ratzinger. The whole sentence reads as follows: "ridding himself of all slavery to the passions, [man] presses forward toward his goal by freely choosing what is good, and, by his diligence and skill, effectively secures for himself the means suited to this end."

In short, what may otherwise be a theologically quite justified will to optimism does not in any case impose upon us the "platitudes of an ethics modelled on that of the Stoa" (138; *LTK*, 332).

Finally, regarding the dialogical or social dimension of existence, paragraph 12 of *Gaudium et Spes* describes the human person as a "social being who essentially exists in relationships." But paragraphs 15–17, which expound the meaning of human spirituality (intellect, conscience, freedom), do not mention the person's essential ordination to love. They do not do so, Ratzinger says, probably because of "the method of composition, which assigned the social phenomenon as a whole to Chapter II" (131; *LTK*, 325–26). He insists that a consequence of this method, nevertheless, is that the constitutive character of the I-Thou relationship for human existence does not stand out as clearly as it could have. "The concept of the personal factor is . . . almost completely lacking" (131; *LTK*, 326). Furthermore, the discussion of freedom in paragraph 17 concerns itself mostly with freedom of choice. The discussion does not treat sufficiently the ontological meaning of freedom as living "in the presence of God" and, consequently, as truly understandable only in terms of this relation to God.

Ratzinger's commentary on the concluding paragraph of Chapter I of *Gaudium et Spes* makes clear the deeper source of the tensions he perceives in the document, as well as the way toward their resolution. In paragraph 22, we find the well-known text: Jesus Christ, "in the very revelation of the mystery of the Father and of his love, fully reveals man to himself and brings to light his most high calling."[7] Pointing to this text, Ratzinger says that "the chapter on the dig-

---

7. Cf. Henri de Lubac, *Catholicisme* (Paris: Cerf, 1938): "In revealing the Father and being revealed by him, Christ completes the revelation of man to himself" (264). To my knowledge, British theologian Paul McPartlan was the first to point out the near identity between the text of de Lubac and that of *Gaudium et Spes*. Pope John Paul II notes his collaboration with de Lubac regarding Schema 13, their agreement, and the friendship begun between them at this time, in *Crossing the Threshold of Hope (CTH)* (New York: Knopf, 1994), 159.

nity of man culminates in Christ, who is now presented as the true answer to the question of being human, and therefore to the questions of true humanism and of atheism" (159; *LTK*, 350). Through our incorporation into Christ, we become sons and daughters in the Son. Thus, concludes Ratzinger, "we are probably justified in saying that here for the first time in an official document of the Magisterium a new type of completely christocentric theology appears." A document whose anthropology appears at first too humanist in tendency culminates in the idea of adoration: man "is only in possession of himself when he has gone forth from himself: Abba, Father" (163; *LTK*, 354).

The concrete path to be followed by nature, in order to realize its identity as nature, is therefore revealed by God Himself in Jesus Christ, and by the mysteries of faith entailed in this revelation. John Paul insists that an organic union of theocentrism and anthropocentrism is "one of the basic principles, perhaps the most important one, of the teaching of the last Council."[8]

Significantly, the *Catechism of the Catholic Church* reflects this shift in its first and basic statement about the dignity of the human person as the image of God, which begins with *Gaudium et Spes* 22 and not *Gaudium et Spes* 12.[9] The *Catechism* understands the *imago Dei* from the beginning as the image of God in Christ and as disfigured by sin. The *Catechism* emphasizes that "the divine image is

---

8. *Dives in Misericordia*, no. 1; cf. *RH*, nos. 1–12. As is well-known, *GS*, no. 22, is cited prominently in virtually all of the Pope's encyclicals. Cf. also here the comment in *CTH*: "[The Council's] teaching is christocentric in all of its aspects, and therefore it is profoundly rooted in the Mystery of the Trinity" (137). To avoid misunderstanding, it should be emphasized that the Pope's christocentrism is not a "christomonism": Christ is always viewed in relation to the Father and the Spirit (hence my use of the term, "trinitarian christocentrism").

9. Cf. no. 1701: " 'Christ, ... in the very revelation of the mystery of the Father and of his love, makes man fully manifest to himself and brings to light his exalted vocation' [*GS*, no. 22]. It is in Christ, 'the image of the invisible God,' [Col. 1:15; cf. 2 Cor. 4:4] that man has been created 'in the image and likeness' of the Creator. It is in Christ, Redeemer and Savior, that the divine image, disfigured in man by the first sin, has been restored to its original beauty and ennobled by the grace of God [cf. *GS*, no. 22]."

present in every man" and that "it shines forth in the communion of persons, in the likeness of the union of the divine persons among themselves" (no. 1702).

Thus, John Paul has emphasized a trinitarian and christological — as distinct from merely theistic — understanding of the *imago Dei,* and he has done so with the explicit intention of retrieving the authentic meaning of Vatican Council II. In the name of the Council, the Pope has offered a new — or renewed — understanding of man in terms of God, the concrete trinitarian God revealed in Jesus Christ.

The human being is never neutral toward God, in any of his thoughts or actions. In the more abstract language of the modern tradition, there is no "pure" nature untouched by grace. There is only a human nature always-already restless for God and burdened by sin.

To put it another way, the person is most profoundly defined by his or her capacity for God. Human existence is a dramatic engagement with God, and this engagement is (ontologically) prior to, and always somehow conditions the person's involvement in, moral, economic, and political affairs.

In his christocentric reading of the *imago Dei,* John Paul offers a new defense of the integrity of nature, already at the level of nature. The Pope's anthropological achievement comes not only by way of "supernatural addition" to the "natural," as it were, but already affects what is meant by nature.

This does not mean that the theo- or christocentric way of understanding nature confuses the orders of nature and grace. The model is "assumption" and not "absorption" (*GS,* no. 22). The point, simply, is that deepening relation to God in Jesus Christ is necessary — in the one and only order of history — for the deepening integrity of nature.[10] The relation between God and the integrity of nature, in

10. The movement toward God can, of course, be implicit. The point is that nature is never neutral or indifferent toward God, and hence that any authentic deepening of the integrity of nature always at least implies movement toward

other words, is not inverse but direct; it is mutual but asymmetrical; that is, nature realizes its integrity, as nature, not by remaining in a state of juxtaposition to God, but by being taken ever more comprehensively and profoundly into union with God. All aspects of human life, thought, and action are intended to have the "look" or "form" of the trinitarian *communio personarum,* of the *fiat* and the *magnificat,* and of the Eucharist. Needless to say, this "con-formation" is primarily the work of the Holy Spirit.

Here, then, is the origin of the universality of the call to holiness: all human beings are called at their creation to communion with the God of Jesus Christ, a communion that is first actualized at baptism. This call to communion reveals the vocation that ultimately defines man. The implication is stunning: Christ, as the "new man" (*GS,* no. 22), reveals what the human person most truly is, in grace — what he is called from his beginning to become. We realize our identity as persons finally only by "putting on Jesus Christ."

Here also is the radical origin of the missionary task actually handed on at baptism: to be made in the image of God in Christ is to be made in the image of the One who is sent (*missio*) by the Father to enter and transfigure the world, in order to return the world to the Father. In other words, as emphasized in the Church's *Ad Gentes Divinitus* (no. 2) and repeated by John Paul in *Redemptoris Missio* (no. 1), the missionary task begins ultimately in the procession of the Second Person of the Trinity, which takes its "economic" form in Jesus Christ — the Jesus to whom our lives are called to be conformed by the power of the Spirit ("I live now, not I, but Christ lives in me," Gal. 2:20).

In sum, the remarkable shift occurring in John Paul's anthropology is revealed especially in his anchoring of the call to holiness, and indeed to mission, already in the primitive

---

rather than away from God, even if God is not explicitly known or intended. Cf. *Nostra Aetate,* no. 2; *Lumen Gentium,* no. 16.

identity of each human person. Not to become holy, not
to fulfill one's missionary calling, is to fail to realize the
destiny that, at the most profound level, defines one's very
self. It is more accurate to say that mission is something
I already am than something I will eventually have. Consequently, mission is not something that I may choose to
engage only part-time or not at all, without significant loss
to my personal identity.[11]

The *"New Evangelization"* and *Today's Cultural Situation*

In speaking of the need for a renewal of the Church's
missionary task, the Pope in *Redemptoris Missio* (RM)
distinguishes three different situations: first, a situation requiring mission in the traditional sense — to those peoples
who have not yet heard the Gospel preached; second, a situation more properly requiring pastoral care: having been
"successfully" evangelized, cultures in this situation now
require mostly the "ordinary" work of the sacraments; finally, a third or "intermediate" situation, which the Pope
says calls for a "new" or "re-" evangelization: one wherein
"entire groups of the baptized have lost a living sense of
the faith or... live a life far removed from Christ and his
Gospel" (*RM*, no. 33).

The Pope insists on the ambiguity of this intermediate
cultural situation. Coincident with "people sinking ever
deeper into consumerism and materialism," our times witness "a desperate search for meaning [and] for an inner
life" (*RM*, no. 38). Even "in secularized societies the spiritual dimension of life is being sought after as an antidote
to dehumanization" (*RM*, no. 38).

---

11. The claim here is as delicate as it is complex. Only in Jesus Christ can there
be a simple identity between person and mission. In creatures, this identity is at
once an always-already offered gift (grace proper to the order of creation) and a
gift yet to be realized (grace proper to the order of justification and redemption).

Elsewhere, in *Evangelium Vitae* (*EV*), the Pope characterizes the current cultural situation in terms of a contrast between the "culture of life" and the "culture of death": "[The present] situation, with its lights and shadows, ought to make us all fully aware that we are facing an enormous and dramatic clash between good and evil, death and life, the 'culture of death' and the 'culture of life.' We find ourselves not only 'faced with' but necessarily 'in the midst of' this conflict" (no. 28).

America represents the "intermediate" situation identified by the Pope as needing a "re-evangelization." Its cultural situation is helpfully illuminated by the contrast between the "culture of life" and the "culture of death." America's cultural problems are primarily theological-religious in nature. This is why America needs a "new or re-evangelization," that is, a renewal of the Gospel more than of individual or social ethics (though of course the former renewal includes the latter).

The Theological Nature of the New Evangelization

John Paul understands the most urgent problem of our time to be the "death" of God, which takes a practical as well as a theoretical form.[12] The "materialism, individualism, utilitarianism, and hedonism," which he sums up as the "culture of death," are all a function finally of "the eclipse of the

---

12. Cf. the Pope's comments in *CTH*, where, citing André Malraux, he says that "the twenty-first century [will] be a century of religion or it [will] not be at all" (228–29). Note also *CTH*, 132–33, where he discusses the fall of Communism and the fact that it still leaves us with problems of "power structures and structures of oppression, both political and cultural (especially through the media)" (132). The cause of these problems — illustrated, for example, by "the increasing gap between the rich North and the ever poorer South" (133) — lies in "the struggle against God, the systematic elimination of all that is Christian. This struggle has to a large degree dominated thought and life in the West for three centuries" (133). Of course we will have to discuss whether the "struggle against God" accurately identifies the nature of the problem in North America — that is, in the face of the empirical-polling evidence that suggests continuing widespread belief in God.

sense of God" (*EV*, no. 23). This is why he calls first for
re-evangelization — as distinct from ethical rearmament —
in response to America's problems.

The culture of death is characterized by a false autonomy
of the self expressed at once in an arbitrary subjectivity or
relativism and a disposition toward control and manipulation or mere "use" of others for pleasure or profit. The
source of this false autonomy is "the loss of contact with
God's wise design" (*EV*, no. 22). "By living 'as if God did
not exist,' man not only loses sight of the mystery of God,
but also of the mystery of the world and the mystery of
his own being" (*EV*, no. 22). Ultimately, only "the blood
of Christ, while it reveals the grandeur of the Father's love,
[can show] how precious man is to God's eyes and how
priceless the value of his life" (*EV*, no. 25).

Thus, for the Pope, what most fundamentally constitutes
our society's tendency toward a "culture of death" is its loss
of a living sense of God's presence as Creator and Redeemer,
and hence of the world as created and redeemed. The Pope
powerfully summarizes this lack of awareness of the gift
character of creation in *Evangelium Vitae:*

> We need first of all to foster in ourselves and in others
> a contemplative outlook. Such an outlook arises from
> faith in the God of life, who has created every individ-
> ual as a "wonder" (cf. Ps. 139:14). It is the outlook
> of those who see life in its deeper meaning, who grasp
> its utter gratuitousness, its beauty, and its invitation to
> freedom and responsibility. It is the outlook of those
> who do not presume to take possession of reality, but
> instead accept it as a gift, discovering in all things the
> reflection of the Creator and seeing in every person his
> living image (cf. Gen. 1:27; Ps. 8:5)....
>
> It is time for all of us to adopt this outlook and
> with deep religious awe to rediscover the ability to
> revere and honor every person.... Inspired by this con-
> templative outlook, the new people of the redeemed

cannot but respond with songs of joy, praise, and
thanksgiving for the priceless gift of life, for the mystery of every individual's call to share through Christ
in the life of grace and in an existence of unending
communion with God our Creator and Father. (no. 83)

The loss of a living sense of God's presence claimed by
the Pope is not measured first in the empirical terms of public opinion polls. On the contrary, these polls tell us that,
in America at least, more than 90 percent of the people still
profess belief in God.[13] What I wish to suggest is that the
Pope is much closer to, say, Nietzsche than to Andrew Greeley in his reading of our current predicament. For Greeley,
America is exceptional in that modernity here has not entailed secularization, as it has in other cultures. The Pope's
implied position is more like that of Nietzsche who, while
recognizing widespread profession of belief and indeed even
relatively full churches, still insisted that God was dead.
What Nietzsche meant, of course, was that God was no
longer alive in the culture; that the infinite no longer gave
depth and form to the being and acting and making of the
finite; that the finite was no longer related to the infinite
within its finite activities.

Needless to say, John Paul goes in an opposite direction
from Nietzsche in his response to the theological-spiritual
crisis identified here. Nietzsche seeks to reawaken a living sense of the infinite within the finite by absolutizing

---

13. Cf. George Gallup, Jr., and Jim Castelli, *The People's Religion: American Faith in the 90's* (New York, 1989). Gallup and Castelli contend that "basic
religious beliefs, and even religious practice, today, differ relatively little from
the levels recorded fifty years ago" (4). Indeed, they say, "the baseline of religious belief is remarkably high — certainly, the highest of any developed nation
in the world" (20). In anticipation of the argument to follow, I should stress that
my criticism of American religiosity does not at all call into question what is
often America's deep religious sincerity or indeed abundant moral generosity. On
the contrary, I assume these. My criticism is directed rather at the "ideological
framework," or "logic," which nonetheless often — and largely unconsciously —
undermines this sincere religious and moral intentionality. (Cf., for example, what
I take to be the similar spirit of criticism developed in Will Herberg's classic
Protestant Catholic Jew [Chicago: University of Chicago Press, 1983].)

human creativity. The Pope, on the contrary, reawakens this sense by "relativizing" — that is, "relationalizing" — human creativity by reestablishing the true relation to God that restores the finite to its true creatureliness. And, for the Pope, it is the feminine (Marian) *theotokos* and not the masculine *Übermensch* who shows the way to make God live again in the world.

The problem of this crisis of belief is put well by Alasdair MacIntyre: "The difficulty lies in the combination of atheism in the practice of the life of the vast majority, with the profession of either superstition or theism by that same majority. The creed of the English is that there is no God and that it is wise to pray to him from time to time."[14]

In short, the problem of God's "death" is a problem already among the 90 percent who profess belief in God, presumably sincerely. The problematic lack of a Creator and Redeemer God who is present at the core of one's life and shapes all of one's making and doing begins already in the majority of believers and not merely in religion's cultured despisers. The question that the Pope forces us to face is not the crude one of whether persons explicitly profess belief in God, but the more subtle one of the extent to which even those who do profess such belief themselves see and enact the full implications of God as Creator and Redeemer for the whole pattern of their daily thoughts and actions — that is, again, granting the sincerity of their profession of faith.

The burden of John Paul's call for a new evangelization, in a word, is that, without a genuine renewal of this "seeing," efforts at moral and political and economic reform risk merely reinstating our problems, however much these efforts may bring about external improvements or short-term gains.

---

14. *Against the Self-Images of the Age* (New York: Schocken Books, 1971), 26.

An Authentic Theology of
Integral Human Liberation

The Pope's new evangelization entails a "new" theology of liberation, which he terms "an authentic theology of integral human liberation."[15] Our culture desperately needs moral and social reform, but in the more basic context of liberation from slavery to sin.[16] The primary need is for forgiveness by God and conversion (cf. *Dominum et Vivificantem*), accompanied by a deepened sense of God's mercy (cf. *Dives in Misericordia*).

The appeal to an "authentic theology of liberation" sharpens our understanding of how sin is the radical source of today's cultural difficulties. Recall Ratzinger's insistence on the need to distinguish between dominion and the capacity for worship as the primary content of the *imago Dei* and to conceive the moral capacities of human freedom from the beginning within the deep discord that runs through man on account of sin. Ratzinger's insistence in both cases bears on the proper relation between God and man in man's basic moral achievement. The neuralgic question is whether God or man is first in that achievement. The issue bears precisely on whether — in what sense — we are first "receivers" or first "achievers."

To put it in a word, the risk, if we neglect the theological-spiritual for the moral or social context of reform, is that we will succeed in putting into place merely another version of the same falsely "constructive" — Pelagian, or at best semi-Pelagian — self that is the source of the problem. In short, liberation from sin is the necessary anterior-immanent condition for all authentic moral and social-political reform. This is perhaps the most fundamental implication of the Pope's shift to a genuinely christocentric understanding of the *imago Dei*.

---

15. *Centesimus Annus*, no. 26.
16. Cf. *ICFL*, nos. 62–65, 71–72, 99, and passim; *CTH*, 69–76; 54–59; *Reconciliatio et Paenitentia*, no. 2.

The full meaning of sin is not understood unless we have distinguished with John Paul the subjective or interior dimension of sin from its objective or external dimension. Thus, as the Pope puts it in *Dominum et Vivificantem:*

> Unfortunately, the resistance to the Holy Spirit which Saint Paul emphasizes in the interior and subjective dimension as tension, struggle, and rebellion taking place in the human heart finds in every period of history and especially in the modern era its external dimension, which takes concrete form as the content of culture and civilization, as a philosophical system, an ideology, a programme for action and for the shaping of human behavior. (no. 56)

The distinction indicated here is developed by John Paul in terms of "structures of sin."[17]

Three qualifiers enable us to understand this notion properly. First, structural or social sin is essentially linked with personal sin: it is "the result of the accumulation and concentration of many personal sins."[18] The institutions and structures of society, abstracted from individual persons, cannot be the proper subject of moral acts (*Reconciliatio et Paenitentia*, no. 16). Second, within sin we must nonetheless distinguish between its "subjective" and its "external" or "objective" dimension, the latter dimension consisting in a false philosophy or view of reality. Sin, in other words, is at once a matter of (subjective) will and (objective) intelligence. Finally, and in light of these two qualifiers, it is necessary and sometimes extremely important for us, when analyzing cultural situations, to speak of sin as extended or consolidated into societal structures.[19]

---

17. Cf. *Sollicitudo Rei Socialis* (*SRS*), nos. 36–37; *Reconciliatio et Paenitentia*, no. 16; *ICFL*, no. 75. Cf. also, for example, *Centesimus Annus*, no. 38, and *Evangelium Vitae*, no. 12, where the notion is used in the Pope's own cultural analysis.
18. *Reconciliatio et Paenitentia*, no. 16.
19. *Sollicitudo Rei Socialis*, no. 36.

The presupposition of the foregoing is that the notion of "structural sin" can be properly applied to Western liberal societies. Now, many are disposed to question this, for what is often claimed as the uniqueness of these societies, at least in their Anglo-American version, is that they have no ideology,[20] officially speaking. The genius of Anglo-American society, it is claimed, lies in the fact that its freedom, or its institutional structures, strictly speaking, are empty of ideology. This view is most often associated, in Catholic circles, with the work of John Courtney Murray, who characteristically insists on the "exceptionalism" of American liberalism. Peculiar to the American liberal tradition, according to Murray, is its ability to distinguish cleanly between the institutional structures proper to the state on the one hand, and the various ideologies proper to society on the other. Murray's sense of this distinction is enshrined in his "articles of peace" reading of the First Amendment.[21]

John Paul's emphasis upon sin in both its "subjective" and its "structural" dimensions as a fundamental category in analyzing the contemporary cultural situation demands that we scrutinize this conventional distinction between lib-

---

20. The term "ideology" as used throughout my essay is (roughly) synonymous with "philosophy" or "worldview" — with any substantive claim, in short, that bears on the nature of human existence and destiny.

21. John Courtney Murray, *We Hold These Truths* (New York: Sheed and Ward, 1960), esp. chap. 2, 45–78. Cf. also in this connection John Rawls's *Political Liberalism* (New York: Columbia University Press, 1993), which distinguishes between "political liberalism" and "comprehensive liberalism": "Political liberalism is not comprehensive liberalism. It does not take a general position on [basic questions of moral epistemology: the nature and source of moral knowledge], but leaves these questions to be answered in their own way by different comprehensive views" (xxvi). "Which moral judgments are true, all things considered, is not a matter for political liberalism . . . " (xx). Rawls then goes on to acknowledge that some position regarding moral epistemology must nonetheless be assumed as part of the background culture needed to support a constitutional democratic regime, and he refers to Hume and Kant as examples of the sort of position required (xxvi–xxviii). But it is just the crucial ambiguity indicated here — on the one hand, no substantive moral philosophy proper to liberal institutions as such, which bear only the "empty" form of justice; on the other hand, and at the same time, presupposition of a substantive moral philosophy as the "background doctrine" necessary to sustain this "empty" form of justice — that it is the burden of the following argument to expose.

eral institutional structures and ideology; in other words, we must ask whether, even (also) in the case of America, a clean distinction between structures and ideology has obtained, and hence whether America (in contrast, for example, to nonliberal and indeed European liberal nations) is without "structural sin."

John Paul does not deny the distinction between political-institutional structures and ideology — on the contrary, he explicitly affirms it (see, for example, *Centesimus Annus,* nos. 36, 39). The point rather is that he understands the distinction differently from American liberals (including sophisticated Catholic-conservative liberals like Murray). The difference lies in John Paul's conceiving the distinction between structures and ideology in terms of an intrinsic rather than extrinsic relation. Although political structures and ideology may be distinguished, there is no actual political structure that is not always-already unified with some ideology. How is this so?

Both Thomists and Cartesians insist, for example, on a real distinction between soul and body. For the Thomist, however, the body is never an empty shell (machine) awaiting the human meaning given by the soul. On the contrary, the body is always-already informed with this meaning, and hence filled with implications relative to the true end of human existence.

Something analogous happens in the case of human institutions, which, after all, are but extensions of the human being. These institutions as such, that is, already in their "external" or merely "physical" aspects, are in a significant sense "ensouled," and hence always-already pregnant with implications regarding human destiny. Thus, the conventional American liberal way of distinguishing between political structures and ideology is more Cartesian than Thomistic — and so inconsistent with the Pope's thinking.[22]

---

22. Cf., for example, John Locke's *A Letter Concerning Toleration* (New York: Macmillan/Library of Liberal Arts, 1950), which makes clear that there

The burden of my argument is thus twofold: first, the claim of an empty institutional shell (cf. Murray's "articles of peace") itself already implies a(n) (substantive) ideology,[23] and, second, the implied ideology is "bad" — it already itself instances the beginning of sin in its "objective" or "structural" sense.

The latter claim may seem strong, but we have seen that a (simple) dualism between political structures and ideology is already unacceptable. The further implication of this claim is that such dualism puts political institutions as a matter of principle on the road to "proceduralism." That is, political-legal institutions whose hallmark is neutrality with respect to ideology (cf. "articles of peace") tend, insofar as they act with consistency, to favor neutrality in their official decisions. They tend — again insofar as they act consistently in terms of their (putative) ideological emptiness — to act as referees whose purpose is solely to keep the societal playing field level, by insuring the equal freedom of all individual citizens to choose and to protect their rights. What this implies is that such political-legal institutions tend always to act in favor of the (empty) form of freedom and never in favor of the (substantive) ideology of any person or group in society. Hence "proceduralism": "form" as a matter of principle displaces "substance" in society's official-legal workings.

The paradox implied by this proceduralism is clear: the claim of an ideologically empty institution is itself already an expression of ("Cartesian") dualism. That the paradox

---

is an intrinsic connection between a state (political structures)-society (ideology) dualism and a body-soul dualism (cf. Patrick Romanell's comments in his introduction to this Liberal Arts edition, regarding the Cartesian inheritance of Locke's conception, p. 9).

23. If the distinction between political structure and ideology itself presupposes a substantive anthropology, then the claim of an empty political structure, a structure in principle neutral toward all substantive anthropologies, is in principle self-refuting. In the words of Alasdair MacIntyre, end of ideology arguments themselves always instantiate "the end of the end of ideology." Cf. his "The End of Ideology and the End of the End of Ideology," in *Against the Self-Images of the Age*, 3–11.

is pernicious can be seen in light of *Evangelium Vitae*'s reference to the threat of an inversion of democracy into totalitarianism (cf. no. 20). Proceduralism in the end renders society incapable, officially-publicly, of supporting any ideology but that of the equal freedom of individuals to choose (which freedom, again, is enforced not as an ideology but only as a "form"). All would-be debates in the legal-public order regarding substantive truths inevitably give way to conflicts over the form of competing freedoms.[24]

The resulting "totalitarianism" is real, however much it remains largely invisible. Indeed, this totalitarianism is potentially all the more pernicious because it remains invisible. What is peculiar to totalitarianism of the "democratic" or "procedural" sort is that citizens remain "physically" free — indeed, almost absolutely so — even as they are no longer able to give any substantial content to their freedom when in public.[25] They are no longer able, that is, to embody

---

24. Not surprisingly, these conflicts thus drift invariably toward "judicial" rather than "truth-ful" resolution: thus Alasdair MacIntyre says that the "lawyers, not the philosophers, are the clergy of [the liberal society]" (cf. *Whose Justice, Which Rationality?* [Notre Dame, Ind.: University of Notre Dame Press, 1988], 344). It is interesting to recall in this connection that Murray, in the context of his defense of an "articles of peace" reading of the First Amendment, praises just this lawyerly quality of the American regime as essential to the regime's distinctive genius: cf. *We Hold These Truths*, 56, 77.

25. Cf. in this connection what Alexis de Tocqueville noted as the peculiar threat of a "tyranny of the majority" in (American) democracy: "Formerly tyranny used the clumsy weapons of chains and hangmen; nowadays even despotism, though it seemed to have nothing more to learn, has been perfected by civilization.

"Princes made violence a physical thing but our contemporary democratic republics have turned it into something as intellectual as the human will it is intended to constrain. Under the absolute government of a single man, despotism, to reach the soul, clumsily struck at the body, and the soul, escaping from such blows, rose gloriously above it; but in democratic republics that is not at all how tyranny behaves; it leaves the body alone and goes straight for the soul. The master no longer says: 'Think like me or you die.' He does say: 'You are free not to think as I do; you can keep your life and property and all; but from this day you are a stranger among us.... You will retain your rights, but they will be useless to you' " (*Democracy in America* [New York: Doubleday Anchor, 1969], 255f.).

For this reason, Tocqueville says: "I know no country in which, generally speaking, there is less independence of mind and true freedom of discussion than in America" (254f.). And again: "What I find most repulsive in America is not the extreme freedom reigning there but the shortage of guarantees against tyranny" (252).

the substance of their views regarding the human person and God in the institutions of society, insofar as these latter are affected by the official-legal power of the state. The nature of this "procedural totalitarianism" can perhaps be best illustrated with reference to issues surrounding life and the integrity of the family: abortion, same-sex marriages, reproductive technology, cloning, and the like. In debates over these matters, the very introduction of normative questions concerning the substantive meaning (and destiny) of the human person, of human dignity, and of gender is viewed increasingly as a matter, *eo ipso,* of undemocratic intolerance.[26]

The matter, indeed, is a complex one. The minimal — but basic — point is that it is not true to say that, because the Pope makes a distinction between structures and ideology, he therefore agrees with American liberalism (even in its best expressions, such as that of Murray) regarding the nature of this distinction.

The Marian Dimension of Anthropology

If the problem of our time is the "death" of God, hence the separation of earth from heaven, the required response from earth is a matter first not of "doing" but of "receiving." The only way truly to bring heaven to earth is the way of Mary, in her reality as *theotokos:* "letting God be in us" (*fiat*), in order that we may magnify His presence (*magnificat*).

---

26. Herbert Marcuse was not entirely mistaken regarding his notion of "repressive tolerance" in democratic societies: see his "Repressive Tolerance," in R. P. Wolff, B. Moore, Jr., and H. Marcuse, *A Critique of Pure Tolerance* (Boston: Beacon Press, 1969), 81–123. The intolerance proposed by Marcuse as a response, however, reveals a serious failure to go the genuine roots of the problem. And cf. also in this connection the often profound remarks of Roberto Unger, in *Knowledge and Politics* (New York: Free Press, 1975), regarding the peculiar-paradoxical way in which liberal thought enslaves the mind. But again, from the perspective of the Pope, Unger's discussion of the metaphysical-religious problem of the universal and particular — whose resolution Unger rightly sees as "the necessary basis of every attempt to move beyond liberal thought and the modern state" (290) — fails also to go to the theological roots of the problem.

There is an important link between John Paul's "new evangelization" and "authentic theology of integral human liberation," on the one hand, and his call for a "new feminism" rooted in the distinct "genius of women"[27] and his emphasis on Mary,[28] on the other. This pontificate's new orientation is perhaps best summed up in the priority that the *Catechism* accords the Marian dimension over the Petrine dimension in the Church, in the order of holiness (CCC, no. 773). In short, the new evangelization calls above all for new saints, and the shape of sanctity is first Marian.

The point here is sharpened by recalling again Ratzinger's distinction between dominion and the capacity for God as the primary content of the *imago Dei*. As already indicated, this distinction entails recognition of the primacy of the contemplative in the human being, in relation to God and to God's gift of creation (cf. *ICFL*, no. 34). The importance of this primacy in dealing with the "culture of death" is underscored in the text cited earlier from *Evangelium Vitae* (no. 83).

Thus, the key problem in the "culture of death" is its false autonomy or "constructiveness" of the self in relation to God and neighbor. This false autonomy can be best identified in terms of Pelagianism and, at the same time, of a "contractualist" (or "nominalist") notion of relation. That a Pelagian tendency is characteristic of the Enlightenment stream of the American culture hardly requires argument.

---

27. Cf. *Mulieris Dignitatem*, no. 11; "Letter on Women," nos. 9–12; *Evangelium Vitae*, no. 99.
28. Cf. *ICFL*, nos. 97–98, and *Redemptoris Mater*, no. 37, where the centrality of Mary for the "new" liberation theology is made clear: "Mary is totally dependent on her Son and completely directed toward Him by the impulse of her faith; and, at His side, she is the most perfect image of freedom and of the liberation of humanity and of the universe. It is to her as Mother and Model that the Church must look in order to understand in its completeness the meaning of her own mission" (*ICFL*, no. 97; cf. *RM*, no. 37). "Thus, a theology of freedom and liberation that faithfully echoes Mary's Magnificat preserved in the Church's memory is something needed by the times in which we are living" (*ICFL*, no. 98). And cf. *CTH*, 45: "A Marian dimension and Mariology in the Church are simply another aspect of the Christological focus."

It is helpful here to recall the claims regarding American religiosity made by Will Herberg, in his classic *Protestant Catholic Jew*, and (somewhat differently) by Max Weber, in *The Protestant Ethic and the Spirit of Capitalism (PESC)*.[29] Weber states: "This, the complete elimination of salvation through the Church and the sacraments (which was in Lutheranism by no means developed to its final conclusion), was what formed the absolutely decisive difference [of Puritanism] from Catholicism" (*PESC*, 104).

Fundamental to the Calvinistic-Puritan tradition as described by Weber is its doctrine of predestination coupled with its elimination of salvation through the Church and the sacraments. These together led the Puritan to the question of whether there were any criteria by which membership in the *electi* could be known (*PESC*, 110). Appropriate worldly conduct answered this need for criteria: intense worldly activity "alone disperses religious doubts and gives the certainty of grace" (*PESC*, 112); good works become "the technical means not of purchasing salvation, but of getting rid of the fear of damnation" (*PESC*, 115). In a word, the Puritans succeeded, where the Catholics had not, in rationalizing the world, through their elimination of "magic" (that is, priestly absolution, transubstantiation) as the means to salvation (*PESC*, 117).

It is difficult to exaggerate the importance of the cultural implications of the inversion occurring here. The Protestant tradition starts out with *sola gratia* and ends up, in Puritanism, with a primacy of "works" — of man's "constructive" activity. What produces this inversion, given Puritanism's distinct doctrine of predestination, is its elimination of the Church and, most pertinently, of sacrament. Since God is no longer "infallibly" present anywhere as a "liberating" force in history — this is the fundamental meaning of Church and sacrament — God is no longer

---

29. New York: Charles Scribner's Sons, 1958. It is not necessary to insist that Weber was right in all details of his argument, only that he was right on the decisive point focused upon in my discussion.

present, that is, by virtue of God's own faithful initiative in a community or institution distinct from oneself. It is inevitable that over time one will incline toward constructing his or her own relation to God, at least as a sign of "liberation."

Here is the heart of the collusion between Puritanism and the Enlightenment that Will Herberg termed "secularized Puritanism." What these two traditions have in common, despite their important differences in other respects, is a distant God. One establishes a relationship through voluntary actions. While relation to this distant God may be viewed quite differently by serious Puritans and, say, Deists, the point is that God can be drawn into history, or, better, God's reality in history can be confirmed, primarily through actions *initiated by individual men.*

Thus, from a Catholic perspective, the peculiar religiosity and/or secularism of America is best understood in terms of America's failure to integrate the orders of creation and redemption sufficiently into an adequate notion of the Church. An adequate notion of the Church, on a Catholic reading, hinges on sacrament: on an "infallible" presence of God that presupposes both an "infallible" initiation (by God in Jesus Christ) and an "infallible" reception (by man under the influence of the grace of God in Jesus Christ). The "infallible" initiation is the priestly-hierarchical principle; the "infallible" reception lies above all in the purity of Mary's *fiat* (under the power of the Holy Spirit) and thereby in the abiding Marian dimension of the Church.

In other words, America has a falsely "constructivist" view of the individual self,[30] and this view is linked indissolubly with a false understanding of the transcendence — and simultaneously of the immanence — of God. An ad-

---

30. For helpful further discussions in light of the claim of a "constructivist" self proposed here, cf. John Dewey's *Reconstruction in Philosophy* (Boston: Beacon Press, 1920), where he describes at great length Francis Bacon's dictum "knowledge is power" as a unifying influence in all aspects (science, philosophy, religion, politics, and industry) of American culture (especially 28–52).

equate understanding of this simultaneous transcendence and immanence of God can come, finally, only through the experience of an essentially Marian-sacramental Church.

John Paul's new evangelization, with its Christ-centered *imago Dei,* implies an anthropology wherein the "receptive" rather than "creative" or "constructive" dimension of the self is primary, and this anthropology cannot be realized finally except in and through integration into a truly Marian and sacramental Church. Hence, once again, the importance of the theological-spiritual nature of the evangelization called for by the Pope: anthropological renewal throughout the culture will occur finally only within an ecclesial renewal throughout the culture — and among those who are already "religious."

Natural Law and the "Communion of Persons"

With John Paul's renewed sense of the *imago Dei* comes an integration of the natural law into the law of person or indeed of persons in communion, with God and with each other (*communio personarum*).[31] In the created order, the communion of persons occurs first in the family,[32] understood as the "domestic Church."[33] The needed renewal of an ethics of natural law, therefore, is to take place through a renewal of the communion formed in the family and especially the Eucharist.

The point introduced here recalls Ratzinger's comments on the centrality of the *communio* dimension of the human person, and, more comprehensively, the Pope's sustained reflections on the *communio personarum* and the realities of marriage and family — illustrated, for example, in his teach-

---

31. Cf., *inter alia,* John Paul's discussion of "personalism" as the horizon for his pastoral work and for his books *The Acting Person* and *Love and Responsibility,* in CTH, 199–202. The Pope's personalism, of course, always includes a "communion of persons."

32. *Letter to Families,* nos. 6–9; *Familiaris Consortio,* no. 15; CCC, no. 2205.

33. *Familiaris Consortio,* no. 21; *Lumen Gentium,* no. 11; CCC, no. 2204; *Letter to Families,* no. 19.

ing regarding the "nuptial" character of the body.[34] The Pope's teaching in these areas does not imply an elimination of natural law discourse — which would be tantamount to a denial of Chalcedonian Christology. It implies rather a reorientation of natural law discourse, in terms of the relations to God and other creatures that are constitutive of the human person.

The community indicated here is not vaguely communitarian but quite concrete and specific. It is the community initiated by God and first formed with God; and, among men, it is the community that takes its first form in the relations of marriage and family, which relations themselves are an icon of the Church (hence again the family as "domestic church"). Indeed, the teaching of John Paul is truly radical on this point: the whole order of "created grace" — the whole of cosmic order — takes its deepest and most proper meaning from the spousal relation that God has established in Christ with his Church (cf. Ephesians 5).[35]

Natural law discourse, therefore, in light of the Pope's "new" Christ-centered anthropology, needs to be integrated from the outset from and toward the realities of community and love as found first in the family — with its concrete relations of gender, of paternity, maternity, childlikeness, and so on — and (especially) in the sacramental Church of which the family is the domestic version.[36] The pertinent point, relative to the suggestion above about contractualism, is that the most fundamental forms of community and love among men have their roots already in the structure of being, and hence are first "ontological" in nature. The relations constitutive of these forms of community are not actualized and

---

34. Cf. John Paul II, *Original Unity of Man and Woman* (Boston: St. Paul Books and Media, 1981), 70–77, 106–12.

35. Cf. John Paul II, *The Theology of Marriage and Celibacy* (Boston: St. Paul Editions, 1986), 240–46.

36. Hence the importance for Pope John Paul II of his founding, at the beginning of his pontificate, the John Paul II Institute for Studies on Marriage and Family: cf. *CTH*, 209–10.

hence do not derive in the first instance from the voluntary actions initiated by discrete individuals.

The common ground sought in natural law discussions with others has its true beginning just here, in the constitutive relationality of the self with God and neighbor. It is crucial that this common ground always be conceived concretely and dynamically: as bound up organically with the theological realities of creation and redemption.[37]

The Splendor of Truth

The reality of communion emphasized by John Paul is best expressed in the language of beauty.[38] Hence the phrase *veritatis splendor* as emblematic for the whole of his thought.[39] Human freedom is realized in relation to the truth that is ultimately the personal God revealed in Jesus Christ. A relationship with Christ begins in contemplative (not inactive!) prayer — worship and praise.

The implications for individual and social morality are radical. First, the language of beauty implies an overcoming of "moralism," insofar as our moral acts are first called forth by the attractiveness of the other. Our moral acts are, of course, something for which we ourselves are responsible. The pertinent point, however, is that it is the beauty of the other (Other) that first evokes my response and in a significant sense bears it — like the rays of the sun or the smile of the mother. The flower, itself, blooms, but only as its bloom is called forth by the presence of the sun within

---

37. Cf. the statement of Pope John Paul II in *Redemptoris Missio,* where he insists that the "common ground" sought in any dialogue with others must not be abstracted (wrongly) from the realities of Christ, redemption, and the Church, out of a false fear of "christocentrism" or "ecclesiocentrism" (*RM,* no. 17). It should go without saying that this wrong abstraction can occur in the name of "public theologies" on both the Right and the Left, and not only in foreign (non-Christian) societies but in America.

38. Cf. CCC, no. 1701, where the divine image restored to man in Jesus Christ is described first in terms of its beauty. Cf. also *EV,* no. 83.

39. Recall the discussion by John Paul cited earlier regarding the *opus gloriae* as "the fundamental destiny of every creature" (*CTH,* 18).

it. Similarly, with respect to the child who finally returns the smile of the mother, it is the child who smiles, but only because the love of the mother has already entered the child and opened it up. What is implied by the Pope's linguistic shift is that all of morality is fundamentally like this.

Second, the Pope's new — aesthetic — accent in morality overcomes "voluntarism." Morality is never simply a matter of moral or willful intentions, but always (also) of the objective form of the other.[40] Morality, in other words, and recalling again our earlier discussion, is a matter simultaneously of intelligence and will.[41] It is intrinsically a matter of "seeing" as well as of "doing."

Third, the primacy of the aesthetic-contemplative dimension implies that truth is never our possession, strictly speaking. On the contrary, it is always a gift to be wondered at. We hold on to the truth not by attempting to grasp it fully and to exhaust its meaning, but by indwelling what always transcends us. A truth that we "indwell" rather than "possess," however, is just so far a truth that we can never impose on another — and thus we turn to the question of the relation between truth and freedom, especially religious freedom.

Fourth, the Pope's emphasis on man's constitutive relation to God implies a notion of human nature as related first in a "direct" and "positive" as distinct from "indifferent" or "negative" manner to God. And the Pope's emphasis on man's primarily aesthetic-contemplative nature in relation to God and others entails a notion of truth as intrinsically (also) a matter of love. Freedom, and especially religious freedom, is to be understood from within this context of a primarily positive and aesthetic relation to God and others. Religious freedom, in other words, is to be conceived first

---

40. Cf. *ICFL,* no. 26.

41. It is useful to recall here that this unity of the intellective (cognitive) and the volitional (appetitive) dimensions has always, in the classical understanding, defined the meaning of beauty: cf. Aquinas's "*id quod visum* [cognitive dimension], *placet* [appetitive dimension]" ("that which being seen, pleases").

in the positive terms of man's dynamic constitutive orientation toward God, rather than in the "negative" terms of immunity from coercion by others. And freedom is to be understood first in terms of the love implied in the aesthetic act: wonder at the other, respect for the otherness of the other, "letting the other be" (cf. the *fiat*).

Relative to the problem of the constitutional order of society, then, the Pope's position clearly implies that an "empty" or neutral or "articles of peace" juridical order is not necessary to secure religious freedom for all citizens as a matter of principle — that is, rather than as a matter merely of political prudence.[42] (Indeed, as we have already indicated, an empty constitutional order is not possible — and therefore one has not existed, even in the "exceptional" case of America.) The Pope's point is simply that an order properly conditioned by the truth of communal love would recognize the primacy of an aesthetic-contemplative approach to all relations between man and God and among all men.

It is significant, in light of the argument outlined here, that John Paul typically places his discussions of religious freedom in the context of the missionary task and the call for a "new evangelization."[43] Thus, the Pope says, on the one hand, that "the multitudes have the right to know the full riches of Jesus Christ, riches in which we believe that the whole of humanity can find, in unsuspected fullness, everything that it is gropingly searching for concerning God, man and his destiny, life and death, and truth.... This is why the Church keeps her missionary spirit alive and even wishes to intensify it in the moment of history in which we are living."[44]

---

42. Thus the Pope moves us beyond the preconciliar "thesis-hypothesis" terms of the problem of constitutional order. But the point is that the Pope does not follow Murray's "articles of peace" route either. In fact, the Pope's new terms (of aesthetics and *communio*) move beyond both positions.

43. Cf., e.g., *RH*, no. 12; *RM*, no. 39; *CTH*, 114–15.

44. *RM*, no. 8 (cited from Paul VI, *Evangelii Nuntiandi*, no. 53).

The Pope, nonetheless, insists at the same time that the missionary spirit must always be engaged "in a way that respects consciences" (*RM,* no. 8), and that the Church must always propose and never impose the Gospel (*RM,* no. 39). In sum, the Pope unequivocally affirms the right to religious freedom enshrined in Vatican Council II's *Dignitatis Humanae (DH).* Nevertheless, in so doing, he develops a theoretical interpretation of religious freedom that differs significantly from the interpretation typically assumed in North America.[45] John Paul neither demands an empty juridical order nor does he think it necessary to conceive religious freedom primarily in the "negative" terms of immunity from coercion, even for purposes of juridical order.[46] My argument has been that the key to the Pope's emphasis is his new — aesthetic — understanding of truth (the *imago Dei*) in terms of love. The primacy of truth ties the Pope's position intrinsically to the "traditional" view, even as the notion of truth as love transforms the terms of the traditional position and incorporates the "modern" view, by virtue of love's inherent inclusion of freedom.

The shift and the nuance of the Pope's position in these matters I believe are strikingly expressed in the *Catechism*'s treatment of "the social duty of religion and the right to religious freedom."[47] Beginning with an expression of the duty

---

45. See the thorough and nuanced discussion of *Dignitatis Humanae* by Walter Kasper in his monograph *Wahrheit und Freiheit* (Heidelberg: Carl Winter/ Universitätsverlag, 1988). Note especially Kasper's caution against interpreting the Council's resolution of the problem of religious freedom too much through the lens of the "purely juridical resolution" favored by the North Americans (26), as well as his insistence that the problem of religious freedom can be satisfactorily resolved only in the context of a complete theology of freedom, which was not provided by *DH* itself (39). Regarding Murray and his influence on *DH* in shifting the problem of religious liberty from that of a moral right deriving from the dignity of the human person to the technical-juridical constitutional problem, cf. Kasper's discussion on 21ff.

46. Kasper points out that Bishop Wojtyla criticized the purely juridical approach to the question of religious freedom (with its primacy of the "negative" relation of immunity from coercion) (cf. 26–27).

47. CCC, nos. 2104–9. I am grateful to my friend Thomas Storck for first calling these texts to my attention. Their importance as a hermeneutic of *DH* has not yet received the attention it deserves. I must, however, respectfully but firmly

of all persons " 'to seek the truth, especially in what concerns God and his Church' " (no. 2104, citing *DH*, no. 1), the *Catechism* stresses that this "does not contradict a 'sincere respect' for different religions which frequently 'reflect a ray of that truth which enlightens all men,' nor the requirement of charity, which urges Christians 'to treat with love, prudence and patience those who are in error or ignorance with regard to the faith' " (*DH*, no. 14). In number 2105, the *Catechism* then states:

> The duty of offering God genuine worship concerns man both individually and socially. This is "the traditional Catholic teaching on the moral duty of individuals and societies toward the true religion and the one Church of Christ" [*DH*, no. 1]. By constantly evangelizing men, the Church works toward enabling them "to infuse the Christian spirit into the mentality and mores, laws and structures of the communities in which [they] live" [*Apostolicam Actuositatem*, no. 13]. The social duty of Christians is to respect and awaken in each man the love of the true and the good. It requires them to make known the worship of the one true religion which subsists in the Catholic and apostolic Church [cf. *DH*, no. 1]. Christians are called to be the light of the world. Thus, the Church shows forth the kingship of Christ over all creation and in

---

insist that these texts do not indicate a simple return to the traditional position, as Storck appears to think that they do (cf. his "Catholics and Religious Liberty: What Can We Believe?" *Homiletic and Pastoral Review* [January 1997]: 49–56). On the contrary, these texts presuppose the important shift from a primarily institutional-juridical to a *communio* ecclesiology at Vatican II, and they thereby indicate a new synthesis of traditional and modern, in the way I have indicated.

I might add here that, as twentieth-century Catholic thinkers such as Blondel, Péguy, Bernanos, and de Lubac have all made clear, there is an intrinsic link historically between political "integralism" and churchly "clericalism": both operate still within the horizon of a primarily institutional-juridical ecclesiology. On this, cf. my brief article in the symposium, "Smile When You Say, 'Starbucks,' " in *Commonweal* (November 21, 1997): 15–16. The symposium was in response to Eugene's McCarraher's "Smile, When You say 'Laity': The Hidden Triumph of the Consumer Ethos," *Commonweal* (September 12, 1997): 21–25.

particular over human societies [cf. *Apostolicam Ac-tuositatem,* no. 13; Leo XIII, *Immortale Dei,* no. 3, no. 17; Pius XI, *Quas Primas,* no. 8, no. 20].

In number 2106, the *Catechism* states that nobody "may be forced to act against his convictions, nor is anyone to be restrained from acting in accordance with his conscience in religious matters in private or in public, alone or in association with others, within due limits' [*DH,* no. 2]." These "due limits" are spelled out in number 2109: "The 'due limits' which are inherent in [the right to religious liberty] must be determined for each social situation by political prudence, according to the requirements of the common good and ratified by the civil authority in accordance with 'legal principles which are in conformity with the objective moral order' [*DH,* no. 7]."[48] Since this "right is based on the very nature of the human person," it " 'continues to exist even in those who do not live up to their obligation of seeking the truth and adhering to it' [*DH,* no. 2]." It continues, that is, even when "special civil recognition is given to one religious community in the constitutional organization of a state [*DH,* no. 6]" (no. 2107).

The implications of the shift toward the language of (Christ-centered) beauty is at the heart of the Pope's radical emphasis on dialogue: with atheism, with all groups of people, believers and unbelievers. His Christ-centered universalism recognizes that genuine elements of truth and goodness and indeed sanctity can be found anywhere, and not simply within the confines of the visible Church, even as all of these elements "reflect a ray of that truth which enlightens all men" (*Nostra Aetate,* no. 2; cf. *Lumen Gentium,* nos. 8, 16). Following *Gaudium et Spes,* no. 22, the Pope states that every single "one of the four thousand million human beings living on the planet has become a sharer in Jesus Christ [through the Incarnation] from the moment he

---

48. On the notion of the common good, and the state's responsibility for securing the common good, see *CCC,* nos. 1905–12.

is conceived beneath the heart of his mother" (*RH*, no. 13). In his approach to dialogue, John Paul assumes that there can be no intrinsic conflict between the presupposition of truth and the radical respect due the freedom of the other: because the truth, as love, is always-already full of respect for the other.

Our cultural problem, therefore, is that of a practical atheism that marginalizes, privatizes, and finally trivializes the call to holiness built into every human being (even in America!). This is why John Paul calls for a new evangelization. Becoming religious in the required sense for the Pope implies a deepened sense of sin in both its subjective and objective or structural dimensions; a heightened sense of the Marian implications of Christology; a deepened sense of family and Church as the earthly icons of the trinitarian *communio personarum;* and a "new" emphasis on (christological) aesthetics in our fundamental engagement with all aspects of creation and culture. All of these are essential to the task of evangelization, whose purpose is to begin already on earth the "civilization of love" that will be complete only in heaven.[49]

Thus, Pope John Paul's new evangelization, anchored in the anthropology of *Gaudium et Spes,* amounts to nothing less than a comprehensive presentation of the historical and metaphysical meaning of human existence. It contains "the most integral form of theology, the theology of all the encounters between God and the world" (*CTH,* 58).

---

49. Cf. the description of the "civilization of love" in *Letter to Families,* no. 13.